TEA WITH DAD

Finding Myself in My Father's Life

TEA
with
DAD

❧

Finding Myself in My Father's Life

NANCIE LAIRD YOUNG

GREEN PLACE BOOKS · *Brattleboro, Vermont*

Printed in the United States

10 9 8 7 6 5 4 3 2 1

Green Writers Press is a Vermont-based publisher whose mission is to spread
a message of hope and renewal through the words and images we publish.
Throughout we will adhere to our commitment to preserving and protecting
the natural resources of the earth. To that end, a percentage of our proceeds will
be donated to environmental activist groups. Green Writers Press gratefully
acknowledges support from individual donors, friends, and readers to help
support the environment and our publishing initiative. Green Place Books
curates books that tell literary and compelling stories with a focus on writing
about place—these books are more personal stories, memoir, and biographies.

GREEN
PLACE
BOOKS

Giving Voice to Writers & Artists Who Will Make the World a Better Place
Green Writers Press | West Brattleboro, Vermont
www.greenwriterspress.com

Library of Congress Cataloging-in-Publication Data available upon request.

ISBN: 978-1-9505847-6-5

Cover design by Asha Hossain Design LLC

To Mom and Dad, without whose stories I'd have none
and
To Rachel, Sharon, and Jane, my reasons for everything.

Doubt thou the stars are fire;
Doubt that the sun doth move;
Doubt truth to be a liar;
But never doubt I love.

~ William Shakespeare, *Hamlet*, Act 2, Scene 2

I came to see the damage that was done
and the treasures that prevail
　—ADRIENNE RICH, *Diving into the Wreck*

Contents

PART III

PART IV

PART V

TEA WITH DAD

Finding Myself in My Father's Life

Preface

A FEW YEARS AGO, a sudden blizzard in rural Vermont
left me and the relatively few travelers remaining on the
train I had boarded in Newark that morning stranded
for eight hours. Both the main and the backup engines blew after
plowing through too many snowdrifts. The train ground to a
halt just fifteen or twenty minutes from my intended destination
where I had expected to get off the train, jump into a waiting car,
ride to a lovely inn geared toward writers, and spend a week's
vacation focused on mapping out a book based on three hundred
or so haiku I'd written over the past five years.

After many hours of waiting, during which the excellent
Amtrak staff rationed power and fed us snacks of packaged
cookies, chips, and bottled water—in between shifts of trying to
physically dig us out—an engine was sent from the south to push
our train to the side of the main track in order to free the rails for
other traffic long enough to allow time for another train to arrive
to pull us back onto the main track.

Through that experience I learned the etymology of the word
sidetracked, experienced its literal meaning, and began to realize
how being sidetracked functioned both negatively and positively
in my life.

Eight hours later, the train was moving again, but my destination station was closed and there was no one to meet me. The conductor and I agreed I would disembark in Montpelier, where I'd had enough foresight before my phone battery died to request that my daughter make a hotel reservation for me. I'd arrange for travel back to the inn the next day.

Of the four women staying at the inn that week, three of us had difficulties arriving on time due to the storm, so our host announced that rather than meet for readings the first evening, we'd all get a good night's sleep, and after a full day's work the next day, we would gather after dinner to hear what each of us had written.

I followed the group into the Gertrude Stein Salon that first evening and plopped onto the sofa across from the beautiful fire before asking, "What readings?"

I am not sure any of us had read the fine print on the inn's website as we all seemed surprised and somewhat intimidated at the prospect of reading what we had written. *Especially* in early drafts. One of the women, my friend Jerilyn Dufresne, with whom I'd planned this retreat, was working on her latest cozy mystery, another was writing an autobiographical novel, and the fourth member of our group planned to gather everything she knew about the trauma she and many women in theater—and the entertainment industry as a whole—had experienced and shape it into some form.

I moved off the main track I'd been on with the haiku book. I could not imagine standing up in front of my friend and these strangers to read a selection of haiku, so I went to bed, got up the next day, and stared at the white screen of my laptop. Then I began to write.

That evening, I read an essay (now a chapter in this book) about the promise I had made to my dying mother to write and deliver her eulogy. I had not anticipated writing that piece or even thinking about that painful memory. I never expected that I could stand in front of anyone to read something so raw and personal. But I did it. Though a very personal experience for me, it seemed to resonate for the others.

For the next week, I put aside my stack of haiku index cards and for at least eight hours a day, sometimes more, I excavated, prodded, and pushed out words, phrases, sentences, and paragraphs that described feelings and experiences long buried in my memory. What I wrote revealed that though I'd been chugging along for some time (some would say successfully), I was far from the destination I'd planned for my life. I began to see my life much like the train ride I'd just been on—a long trip with obstacles in the way of moving forward and times I moved from one track to another to rest, recover, or sometimes reconsider my destination.

That's how I came write this book, but it does not explain the form it took. My mother's death and my promise to write and deliver her eulogy, the fact that I did not, and the reasons I assigned for that decision all seemed central to my story at the time. But they were not.

Had I known myself better, I wouldn't have made the promise. Had I been in better shape emotionally, I'd have been able to see that the reasons I conjured were part of a personal narrative I'd written over the years about who I was and why I was where I was. I would have seen that my story needed a heavy edit.

At the time I saw myself as a huge failure. From the sidetrack I rested on at that moment, I saw my life's litter on the rails behind me. Two failed marriages, a hopscotch career path, financial problems, and as a sixty-something-year-old woman, I was living with my father. And not because he needed me, but because *I* needed *him*. I wasn't a total loss, but I was pretty much a mess. I could wait for another conductor to call for engines to pull me out, limp along the track I was on—or I could rethink my destination and conduct a new journey myself.

The first stop as I headed out again was to acknowledge and accept that I wanted and needed to have a closer relationship with my father and others. To admit that I needed others. The second was to do the hard work.

I started out slowly and not always smoothly, but eventually I was moving under my own steam again, and this book is about that period of time. Writing about it was part of the process of change, healing, and growth.

There's a certain accountability in writing a scene, seeing yourself as a character in it, and not liking what you see. As the author, one has a chance to change things because there is distance between the page and a tender heart. Enough distance to dull the pain of critique and judgment. Enough space to see that change is possible and that there are ways to go about it. If one can change it on the page, why not in real life?

In my case, the opportunities for insight and change started over afternoon cups of tea with my father. As we talked and shared our stories, we began to drop the assumptions we had about one another. Each of us began to speak more often about how we'd felt at certain times in the past. We became more comfortable expressing those past feelings and the ones we felt now, too. Most importantly, I think, we began to feel more at ease when the other demonstrated feelings. We learned to hear one another and to trust the other to listen.

Yes. That was it. We learned to trust.

Those conversations began to extend into other times—weekend drives, a regularly scheduled dinner date each week, sitting on a bench at the beach and watching the waves.

I'd always wanted to be with my father to care for him in his later years. I know now that we would have muddled through without this time together; but I cannot imagine that we would have been as comfortable, honest, vulnerable, trusting, or demonstrably loving as we are able to be now. I know I would not have been as settled and happy as I am now.

I recommend sidetracking yourself every now and again. The reasons for doing so may not always be positive ones. But there are benefits if one looks for them. Time. Rest. Opportunities to think, to take in the view both behind you and in front of you, and to plan a new way to your next destination.

August 2020

Prologue

Surrender 2013

Five years after I relocated from the Virginia suburbs outside of Washington, DC, to be near my father on Maryland's Eastern Shore, I picked up the phone and heard his voice. As usual, there was no hello. He never says hello when he makes a call, only if he answers one.

"Hi, Dad!" I said.

"Listen. I want to talk to you about something."

My father, a retired U.S. Army full colonel, had used that phrase to open conversations with me while I was growing up and even then, at the age of sixty-one, those words still affected me. My brain, if not my body, stood at attention while my emotions screamed, "*Incoming!*" Then as I struggled to contain the inevitable anxiety that followed, I mobilized as I'd learned to do during my military brat childhood. First, I prepared a defensive position as intel rolled in, just in case one might be in order. Then I held on to my proverbial helmet, hunkered down, and braced myself for what was to come. Curious, yet vigilant.

The past twenty years had been stressful for me; I'd been in "handle what you can, when you can mode" for fifteen of them, which began when my second husband, the person I referred to as my soul mate, the love of my life, disclosed that he was gay. As he and I dealt with that reality while trying to renegotiate our relationship as individuals and parents, I returned to the work-force full-time in my mid-forties after a significant absence. I started a career in the relatively new field of online media (staffed with the very young and brilliant, which I felt did not include me) in order to support my three girls and myself. Then in 2006, my mother died. Two years after her death, I moved (without invita-tion) closer to my father, motivated by the desire to take care of him if he needed me.

My father's call was prompted by, yet again, another of my crises. In typical fashion, I had created and then attempted to deal with too many situations that I wasn't prepared to handle by myself. I'd said nothing when I should have said something. I had not asked for help when I should have. I refused help offered when I should have taken it. Dad was forcing a rescue (whether I had the sense or capacity to ask for one or not). And as he had done several times throughout my life, he intervened just before I hurtled off a cliff.

I ran through all the possible topics Dad might want to dis-cuss. My list of possibilities was long and trailed back to my childhood—possibilities built on a foundation of past situations or recent ones. Yet I suspected that this time money sat at the top of his list. I tried to calculate how many months of rent and utilities I owed him.

~

Earlier that year, my place of work had notified me that they'd received a garnishment notice from the IRS. They calculated that I would be left with only $800 in each monthly paycheck. That wasn't enough to cover rent and utilities, let alone other essen-tials like food, gas, car insurance, phone and internet connections (necessary for my work), medical and dental deductibles, charge account payments, or the college tuition and housing payments for two of my daughters. In addition, my youngest daughter, Jane, attended an out-of-state university and had one semester left to complete before graduation. Then there were the emergencies. I couldn't remember back to a time in my recent history when there hadn't been emergencies.

As the representative from the payroll office read the notice to me, waves of shame and embarrassment almost obscured righteous indignation at the government's lack of consideration for not giving me due notice that they planned to drive me into poverty and demonstrate once again to my father my complete lack of competence at practically everything related to adulting. I swam in a pool concocted of guilt and shame as thick as pitch. I could barely move.

I tried to take comfort in remembering that for the past fifteen years I had survived almost all the experiences on the list of stressors that shorten a human being's life including four of the top five: marital separation, dissolution of the marriage, my mother's death, and a serious medical episode of my own.

Until now I'd escaped imprisonment—number three—since I still had a salary to garnish. I admit now to feeling then that 'three hots and a cot' in a white-collar federal prison environment sounded more appealing than having my father step in. I heard they had libraries and lots of alone time. I fantasized about working out in the prison yard and all the free time I could spend writing.

It would have been simple to resolve the tax issue when it first arose, but instead, overwhelmed about so much for so long, I had thrown the first letter and all subsequent ones into a large plastic box that stood in the corner of my office. I knew the problem wouldn't go away and yet I hoped that, magically, it somehow would. I hoped that something might have been misfiled or calculated incorrectly. Surely, a ridiculous error (on their part) would be discovered, and they'd notify me before I had to sort through boxes of returns and supporting documentation.

After the call from the main office, I dug through the mound of unopened mail I'd thrown in the box of "deal with later" and found all the IRS communications including the warning notice advising me that unless I responded my wages would be garnished. There it was, mixed in with everything else. Later had arrived.

I finally told my father about the situation a few months after I'd used up what savings I'd put away in order to bridge the gap between income and expenses. I had meant to get around to fixing things, but just never managed to do it. I assured Dad it was nothing. I'd take care of it quickly. I knew I didn't owe any taxes—certainly not as much as the IRS claimed—and vowed to fight any penalties and interest due (exponentially more than the alleged taxes owed since I'd delayed so long). Each month I'd write a check to Dad for rent and then ask him to hold it for a week only to call him within a few days to ask him to hold on to it, with all the others, just a bit longer. This process repeated every month for about ten months.

He'd been inordinately patient about my not paying him. He'd been extraordinarily understanding about all my excuses for why I had not connected with the IRS and straightened it out. When he asked, not in a demanding way, but as though he were just interested, I rationalized. I told him I was so busy at work I couldn't get off the phone to call or the lines were always busy when I called during breaks, I needed to talk to them by phone, not just send mail back and forth, I just needed to send them copies of the tax returns in question and I was still looking for them. I knew they were in one of the boxes I hadn't unpacked in five years.

Now, because I had not taken care of or been responsible with my finances, I owed my father thousands of dollars, the last person to whom I ever wanted to owe money. I felt guilty. In addition, I knew my behavior had been inconsiderate and selfish. I was emotionally unequipped to deal with it. I was just *done*. I had shut down.

~

I held the phone to my ear as I walked to the reading chair in my home office—what I considered to be the best room I'd ever had in my whole life—and looked out the sliding glass doors and across the new deck into the pine trees where a squirrel ran up and down a branch. I sat down and threw my feet on the foot stool as though ready for a lovely chat, when the real reason was fear that if I did not sit, I would fall.

I imagined my father on the other end of the line. Was he standing up or sitting in his recliner after having thought this through? Despite his age, my father still stood soldier straight and moved, though more slowly than before, with the same grace of an athlete he'd had his whole life. His formerly platinum-blond hair was turning white now. I could envision him impeccably dressed in his golf shirt and khakis, his clear blue eyes intent on his mission of solving the problem I'd created but had not handled. I waited to hear what he had to say.

It was: "I've decided. You're moving in with me. I'm selling that house."

I felt, then processed, as much as my brain was capable of handling through layers of depression-related numbness. I started to formulate an argument against my father's plan. But for the first time in years—I tried to count how many, but it took too long—my heart recognized and embraced the blessed absence of anxiety and fear. This time I had no desire to prepare a defense or to plead one.

I'd hit bottom. Dad knew it, and now I accepted it, though we had not discussed how bad things were for me then. Any rational being observing me and my life at that time would have seen that it was not just about the taxes. It was about everything, so my response to my father's stepping in this time was different than it had been in the past.

I did not rail against crossed boundaries or parental interference as I had in the past. I did not feel judged. I didn't have the sense of giving up before I did everything I could to remedy the situation. Instead, I felt rescued and trusted that all would be well. I found it uncharacteristically easy to finally loosen my grip from the edge of the roof atop the flaming house of cards I'd been clinging to, trust, and then free-fall into the net he held. I felt only relief. I was grateful someone had intervened. I was glad it was him. I let go and responded without hesitation, albeit weakly: "Okay."

And to myself, I said, "I surrender."

PART I

Coming back is the thing that enables you to see how all the dots in your life are connected, how one decision leads you to another, how one twist of fate, good or bad, brings you to a door that later takes you to another door, which aided by several detours—long hallways and unforeseen stairwells—eventually puts you in the place you are now.

—ANN PATCHETT, *What Now?*

CHAPTER 1

~

Permanent Change of Station

*T*HE MOVE to Dad's house made sense given my situation, but I hated that it was unfolding this way. I had always planned to move closer to him as he aged, but now, rather than a neat segue from living nearby to moving in with him once he could not take care of himself, history was repeating. I had again "gotten myself into so much trouble" that I needed his help. Based on this history, I feared the loss of the ability to make choices for myself. I knew that moving in with Dad was not going to be easy for either of us. If it didn't go well, there was no going back. How do you say, "This isn't working, I'm leaving," to an aging parent who rescued you, especially if you believed you had nowhere else to go?

~

When I packed up and moved closer to Dad in the summer of 2008, two years after my mother's death, I seemed, on most fronts, to be a highly functioning adult. No longer married and an empty nester—one daughter had a family of her own and the other two were away at college—I could run my business as a writer and consultant for online media companies anywhere I could find an internet connection. It made sense to live near him. He was in his late seventies then and in good health, short of slightly high blood pressure. He still worked out daily to remain fit and trim and played eighteen holes of golf every day weather permitting.

But I worried that my father's strength and stamina had been drained after caring for Mom during her last six months of life as they battled her cancer together. I'd wanted to help him if he'd let me should the need arise. Also, I felt even more disconnected from him since Mom's death.

In the beginning I blamed grief, but I began to realize that though grief might be part of it, the long drive from Washington, DC, to his place was not the only distance I had to travel. We didn't really know one another very well anymore, and I sensed a wall between us, built brick by brick, without much notice by either of us, over the course of my life. Mom, I realized then, had moved easily from one side of the wall to the other, sometimes through it, delivering messages, updates, explanations, and translations.

I hoped that living closer to Dad as he aged would facilitate his becoming more comfortable with relying on me. I hoped he'd accept me as a constant part of his life more easily if the move were gradual, rather than if I suddenly descended when he became ill or could not take care of himself. I felt I needed to find a place in his life.

I did not disclose the other reason. I wanted to avoid the mistake I'd made with Mom. I had not spent enough time with her before her death. And the time I had spent had not been saying the things I had needed to say or hearing those things she might have wanted to say to me. Since my mother died, my sense of loss had grown to encompass the fear of even more disconnection from my father and, I was afraid, from my two younger brothers. My family. I wanted as much time as there was left to spend with Dad. I wanted it to be good time, too.

After Mom died, we returned to our old habits of weekly phone calls, though unlike the one- and two-hour calls my mother and I had had, Dad's and mine were short.

"Hi, Dad. How are you?"

"Oh, it's you, Nancie. Just sitting here watching the television. How are you? How are the girls?"

I'd fill him in on the kids' activities and tell him stories I knew would amuse him. He'd listen and then say, "Well, I don't want to keep you. You get back to those girls. Talk to you soon. Love you now. Bye."

I'd stare at the receiver. Our phone calls were more like military briefings.

"All things good? Excellent. Carry on."

I decided that Dad should never spend a major holiday alone. On Thanksgiving, Christmas, Easter, and his birthday, I drove out with at least one or two of the girls in tow (whichever ones were not visiting their fathers), bringing a turkey, potatoes, vegetables, rolls, stuffing, and all the fixings. I'd cook at his house. And since Dad lived so near the beach, we'd spend as many weekends there during the summer that our schedule (and he) would allow.

With the kids' differing and often-competing schedules, let alone Dad's own schedule, I feared it would become harder just to get together, let alone maintain a relationship. I worried that he was aging and lived alone in such an isolated area.

～

A medical emergency tipped the scale in the direction of my decision to live near him on a permanent basis.

Dad called one Sunday afternoon. No hello, of course.

"Guess where I am," he commanded cheerfully.

"I have no idea, Dad. Where are you?" I played along.

"In the emergency room," he answered, as though he were calling to tell me he'd been playing golf and got a hole-in-one.

"Oh my God! What happened? I'll be right out," I told him while my eyes scanned all surfaces in the room for my purse and keys.

"Oh, don't worry, I'm headed home now. I had a nosebleed because of the medicine I've been taking. They cauterized the bleeder. I'll call the doctor tomorrow. I thought you'd want to know," he told me.

"I *do* want to know," I said, "but before you're released! Preferably before you go to the hospital in the first place!"

"You get too worked up," he laughed. "I'm fine."

"Dad, I can be to you in two hours. Two-and-a-half at the most. Please call me when you're ill."

"Yeah, yeah. Have a great night. Just wanted you to know I'm okay."

Later that afternoon, Dad called again.

"Can I take you up on your offer to come out here?" he asked. He sounded weak.

"I'm on my way. What's happening?" My purse and keys were ready since I gathered them right after his last call. I headed to the door.

"My nose is still bleeding, and it's been more than an hour. I can't get it to stop."

"Dad, do you think you need to call an ambulance? I'm on my way, but if you become weak or think you need help, call 911. I'll find you."

"I'm fine. I don't need an ambulance, but I can't drive myself there. Oh, while you're on your way, can you pick me up some chicken nuggets from McDonald's? I haven't eaten all day."

I headed out the door, calling him every fifteen minutes to make sure he was still conscious as well as to gather enough information if I needed to call 911 myself. Except for being hungry and annoyed with me for calling so often, he said he was fine. As I drove east on Route 50, I looked for fast-food drive-thru lines that were short so I could pick up his chicken nuggets.

I found him, lying back in his recliner, his shirt and Bermuda shorts covered with blood. That I was the only one close enough to call is ironic to say the least, since one of the myths in my family is "Nancie's terrified of blood. That's why she didn't become a nurse."

～

A singular bloody episode perpetuated the myth of my alleged fear of blood. It happened at Fort Carson, Colorado, after I returned home from college the summer after my freshman year. My mother and I were in the kitchen making sandwiches when I reached across the clutter on the kitchen counter to grab something. I did not see the empty aluminum can, which was open, its sharp-edged lid standing upright. I didn't feel the slice across my wrist, but I said, "Oh no!" loud enough that my mother turned to see what I described as a "geyser of blood" shooting into the air from my wrist. My mother claimed to have seen only "a little blood" dripping from my wrist onto the floor. The truth lying somewhere in between, there was enough blood that she ran to me and grabbed a dish towel to stem the crimson tide of flowing liquid from my dainty wrist while calling for my father, who ran into the kitchen. At least that's how I remember things before I fainted from all the attention.

As my mother waved smelling salts under my nose, which she always seemed to have handy, I heard my father say, "No guts, no glory, Nancie."

I want to clarify that I am not afraid of other people's blood, just my own, though when my second husband told me that he couldn't handle someone vomiting, I was happy to negotiate the division of responsibilities related to the handling of our children's bodily fluids. I'd take care of wet and dirty diapers as well as their vomit if he would manage bloody injuries. For years, my children would scream as though they were dying when bloody from some fall or encounter with a sharp object, but as we ran to them, they would say, "It's okay, Mom, this one's for Daddy."

As for my having dropped my major in nursing, it had nothing to do with blood. Some other bright and shiny major just caught my attention. That's all.

~

Dad watched me warily from his recliner, seeking any sign that I might faint. "Should I change my clothes first?" he asked.

"No, we can't take the time. Here are your nuggets, Dad. You can eat them as we drive in the car. We're going straight there."

I was angry as I helped Dad to the car—him in his blood-soaked shirt and shorts, with soaked cotton hanging out of his nose, clutching his greasy, scrunched up bag of chicken nuggets. I wanted staff in the emergency room to see the blood on his clothes. I wanted them to reflect on having released my father before they'd fixed the problem and what it had done to him. Also, I knew the sight of that much blood would get us through ER triage faster.

As I suspected, they took us right in to the treatment area after they asked us what the problem was, and I pointed to his bloody clothes.

"He was just here earlier today," I said with rather testy countenance. "His records are probably still up on the screen in there."

Dad and I spent the next few hours behind a curtain waiting for a doctor or nurse to tell us what the problem would be or to give us a sense of how long we'd have to wait. I knew better than to complain. It would have upset Dad. He is a patient man by nature, but his life in the military reinforced this as well as the age-old principle of 'hurry up and wait.' And I knew the nature of emergency rooms, having spent many hours in them given my past experiences as a nursing student and a crisis counselor attending hallucinating, drugged up, or suicidal clients, and my time accompanying rural rescue squads in my earlier lives.

I knew that the nurses, physician assistants, and orderlies weren't sitting around playing cards. They were all occupied with the intake and care of patients or entering the required and necessary information into the computers to assure continuity of quality care. I also knew that we'd arrived during a change of shift, which complicated things a bit more. So when he queried me on what was happening, I just smiled at Dad and shrugged my shoulders with a "what can you do?" attitude, trying to be as calm and as cheerful as I could.

Though Dad's nose still bled, I could tell from reading the machines he was attached to that his oxygen level, pulse, and blood pressure were fine given the situation. Periodically, he would gag as though to vomit. I would put my arm behind him to help him sit up. At first, I was surprised that he accepted my assistance so easily. At one point he vomited a clot that looked like a serving of raw liver. I grabbed a nearby kidney dish, caught it, and discretely moved it to the side cabinet placing a paper towel over it. I laughed to myself as I remembered my famous fainting scene years before. *All guts, no glory in this situation*, I thought.

When the doctor finally pulled open the curtain and walked in, I asked him to look at the clot in the kidney pan that I'd placed on the counter. He lifted the paper towel and asked, "Who left this here?"

"She did," said my father pointing at me. I wasn't sure if it was an accusation or a moment of pride.

By the time Dad was treated and released and I had driven him home, I'd made the decision to move from northern Virginia to be near him. I was determined that he would never be alone in an ER or hospital again. I said nothing of my plans to him because he would have tried to discourage me.

~

Once home, I began to look at real estate ads right away and planned my move. Then one day, Dad mentioned his intention to sell the rental property that he owned in a resort community near Ocean City, Maryland. Before he and Mom had moved from Delaware, this had been the place my brothers and I would visit (with our families) during the summers.

I pounced.

"Dad," I said, "don't sell the house. Rent it to me. You can continue to build equity. I'll restore and update things. It will keep me busy."

He didn't object. I wanted to pay the going rental rate, but Dad insisted on charging only the mortgage payment plus utilities. "I'm not out to make money on this. You're my daughter for God's sake."

It was a good deal. He didn't have to sell an asset. I had a place I could afford to plant myself and putter. We would live close enough to check in on one another with a half-hour distance to maintain our privacy, independence, and emotional space. My father and I share a healthy respect for boundaries.

We called it "the beach house" due to its location in a resort community about six miles from the beach. It rested near a bay separated from the ocean by the main coastal highway. Though our house was not on the bay, it was close to channels that led out to the bay. There were amenities such as a golf course, a yacht club—though I saw many good-sized boats, I never saw a yacht— swimming pools, some shopping and restaurants nearby, and our family favorite, the beach club, which had its own pool, restrooms, and showers, and a cute restaurant to boot. I envisioned many summer reunions with my daughters and their children. It would be easier to nurture family relationships.

It was everything I needed and wanted then. A single-story house with no stair climbing—a relief after the townhouse I'd lived in with my daughters after my ex-husband and I sold the house we'd lived in for the last thirteen years of our marriage. No need to worry about toting heavy laundry baskets, boxes of books, or vacuums up and down flights of stairs. The kitchen was large enough, and with my ex-husband's help, I turned the small breakfast nook across the hall from the kitchen into my office. It was perfect. The window provided a nice view as well as light. The room's size allowed for my two wingback chairs, a lamp table, a bookcase, and a desk with shelves. I would spend about 65 per-cent of my time in that room.

The great room with cathedral ceilings had enough space for both family and dining areas. The screened-in sun porch prom-ised a place for chairs, game table, and daybed for those who wanted to take advantage of the breezes on the large wooded lot. With three bedrooms, I imagined I'd be turning away visitors.

It was also two-and-a-half hours away from my old life. As I had during each change of station the whole time I grew up as a military brat, I viewed the move as a new start. A new me. No looking back, no past sins traveling with me. I could start fresh. Rest. Have time to think. Get my bearings. This time I knew no one, except my father, and I liked it that way. I worked remotely, traveling only if necessary. Outside of my remote work, I maintained contact with friends and family via phone and social media.

For the next five years that I lived in the little "beach house," I maintained my public persona easily. No one local knew me. Business trips and friends' visits were infrequent. I worked hard to present the image of a busy and successful businesswoman with a full-time, work-at-home career not far from the ocean.

I left the house if necessary and then only as proof of life (though selfies worked, too) to shop for food and wine or to visit Dad. Amazon is an enabler for agoraphobes. If they'd delivered groceries back then and I had joined an online wine club, you might be reading a different story.

In the beginning, I enjoyed exploring and getting to know the area. I'd drive to Assateague and walk the beach, hoping to see the horses. I'd stumble upon little ecosystems among the brush and encounter herons or ducks. But after a few visits from some girlfriends and my daughters during the summer, things quieted down. My youngest didn't come out on college breaks. Both transportation and work were easier to find in the DC area where her sisters and father lived. I soon settled into a quiet and solitary routine. My only real contact was Dad a few times a month.

My father always called before dropping by. That gave me enough time to get dressed, clean the house, and appear to be a highly functioning human being rather than the hermetic, perpetually pajama-clad, movie-bingeing, chardonnay-chugging insomniac I had become when I wasn't working.

My innate talent for spin hid the truth—if not from my family and friends, then certainly from myself. It would take me another few years after leaving the beach house and moving in with Dad to admit that my move to the Eastern Shore had not only been motivated by wanting to be closer to him.

I had run away from, but not escaped, the pain and stress related to the end of my second marriage, Mom's death, and every other unresolved issue in my life. I'd merely packed things neatly away and brought them with me to the beach.

CHAPTER 2

~

Packing Up and Moving Out

URING my father's military career, we moved on average every eighteen months. We became expert at breaking camp, packing up, and relocating, and I carried those skills with me after I left home. Though I know I apply them differently than others in my family, those skills and experiences were invaluable when I moved from apartment to apartment while single, out of two marital abodes when my first and second marriages dissolved, and then out to the Eastern Shore.

Still, I'd forgotten what a move with Dad in charge involved, and he'd certainly forgotten what moving with me was like. It had been a long time since he'd tried to herd me through a move. While I tend to focus on the "tell me when we need to be there and I'll be there" approach, Dad attacks a move with the detailed precision and logistical skill of Hannibal planning a crossing of the Alps on African elephants. There's a lot of detail work involved. This time, despite the lessons woven throughout our mutual history, we both entered a state of mind that Samuel Johnson described as "the triumph of hope over experience."

~

I moved out of my parents' home and into my first apartment when I was twenty. I don't count the move into the dorm my freshman year of college as a "move out" since it was only for the school year. The move to an apartment was different. It signaled adulthood and, finally, independence. At least in my mind.

Like every move I'd made before, that one was precipitated by military orders. My father had been reassigned from Fort Carson, Colorado, to the Pentagon in Washington, DC. It was not that I couldn't travel with them or that they didn't want me to. But I was twenty. I had a job. I had friends. I had a Studebaker of my very own worth $250. I did not want to go. I handled the prospect of another move by avoiding the hell out of it.

~

I developed avoidance as a superpower defense mechanism early in childhood, but no one could top my younger brother in that area of expertise back then. When he was a toddler, that kid had been able to self-hypnotize and fall asleep on command. For instance, whenever we were required to receive inoculations, which seemed like all the time, he'd climb up on the exam table at the Post Dispensary and proceed to fall asleep immediately only to wake up just after the doctor withdrew the last needle from his arm or behind when all his shots had been administered. As I stared wide-eyed, both jealous and frightened and on the verge of hysteria, my mother would say, "Oh, Nancie. Stop that, your little brother didn't cry."

No shots were necessary for the move into my first apartment, but when I heard the words, "We've got orders!" I resorted to my arsenal of the move-related, stress-fighting weapons I'd collected over the course of my life.

The announcement of a move when I was a child initiated specific maneuvers. I started the process of readying myself for the changes. I began to pack all my things as well as feelings and anxieties. I walked through the weeks and days before a move ignoring the dread I felt. I would miss my friends, so I distanced myself from them. Who would remember me if we moved all the time? I would have to start over and meet new people. I'd have to start a new school in the middle of the year.

I prayed. A lot. I prayed that someone at the Pentagon had been in a rush and typed my father's name on someone else's orders. But, really, I knew that wouldn't work.

I moved on to asking God to make Mom say she wouldn't move until after the school year ended. It would only delay the move, but it would mean that in February I wouldn't find myself standing in front a class of kids who had been together since at least September as the teacher announced, "Class, we have a new student. I'd like you to meet the new girl, Nancie. That's N-a-n-c-*I-E*., not *Y*. Her family just moved here from Timbuktu. Let's welcome her."

My mother tried to help. I was about ten when moving began to affect me.

"I don't want to move," I told my mother one day while she stirred a pot of boiling something she was experimenting with—I think it was oxtail soup because there were round, purplish pieces of meat piled high on a platter. The kitchen in our Fort Monmouth, New Jersey quarters was hot. Strands of Mom's hair stuck to her forehead and the sides of her face. Her cheeks were flushed. I remember her expression, which I interpreted then as one of annoyance directed at me, but realize now with my experience as a mother and grandmother as more likely to have been, "Really? And you think *I* want to move again? Get over it."

Instead, she turned to me, her left hand on the big pot, a wooden spoon in the other, and said, "Why not?"

I wanted to say that I didn't want to leave my grandparents again—they were just across the Verrazzano Bridge in Brooklyn, and we'd been away from them so long while in Germany, but even at that young age I was aware of the tensions and dislike that existed between my mother and her in-laws. I wanted to say that

I didn't know where Georgia was and that what I saw at night on Walter Cronkite's newscasts about the civil rights tensions in the South frightened me. I wanted to say that the most frightening thing in my life was having to go to a new school in the middle of the year. Instead, I said, "I will miss my friends, and they will miss me."

Mom put down her wooden spoon on the table and said, "Nancie. Come here."

She filled up the sink with water. When it was filled almost to the top, she turned off the water, looked at me, and said, "Stick your arm in that sink of water. Wait a while then pull it out."

I did, and she asked, "What happened?"

I stared at the sink. "I don't know," I replied.

"Think," she said.

"I stuck my arm in and it made a hole in the water," I said.

"What happened when you pulled your arm out?" My mother looked at me.

"The water filled the hole where my arm was," I responded.

"Yes. And that is what will happen when we move. You will leave a hole that gets filled in by new people, so your friends won't be lonely. And in Georgia, you'll make a new space and make new friends. You won't miss your old ones."

I heard the entire conversation. I was there. But despite my poor mother's attempt to assuage my concerns, my ten-year-old self heard only part of the lesson she was trying to teach me. I heard that when we moved to Georgia, no one would miss me. Someone else would take my place, and I'd be forgotten. I said nothing to her, but I promised I'd hate moving for the rest of my life. I also promised myself that my children would never move, that they'd never change schools, and, if they absolutely had to, it would not be in the middle of the year.

～

The news of the move to Washington, DC, provoked a new reaction from me. Of course, I didn't tell my parents that. I allowed them to assume I'd fall into line as usual, get my room and all my belongings sorted and ready to pack according to Dad's timeline for moving out. I let them believe that on the date of departure, I would join my two brothers, our dog, and our cat, pile into our two cars, one with a U-Haul attached, and head across the country as we had so many times before.

I never mentioned the upcoming move to my friends or the people at work as I formulated a plan to stay in Colorado Springs because I was not going to move. Not this time.

About three weeks before the movers were scheduled to come, I walked into my place of work and asked everyone, "Does anyone need a roommate or want to get an apartment with me?"

I do not remember what precipitated that action, but desperation and anger at something, or someone, typically propelled me when I needed transport from a current zone of comfort into the unknown. I was relieved when my friend Rosemary said, "I do!"

We began to look for apartments, and soon after, we found a relatively new, two-bedroom, fully furnished apartment in a small, two-story building not far from work. It was managed by a retired couple. It had an indoor pool, and, if I remember correctly, a small gym area where people could lift weights or do floor exercises, though Rosemary and I never used it. I began to draw up a plan for breaking the news to my parents, but before I could, my father forced the issue.

In the evening on the day Rosemary and I signed the lease on the apartment, my father met me at the door when I got home from work. He was angered and frustrated by my procrastination. I had done nothing to get ready for the move.

"Just when do you think you'll get your things ready for the movers? They'll be here in two weeks. You've done nothing to prepare. If you don't handle this, I will."

I summoned up all my courage and tried to look cool and collected. "Oh, I'm not going," I said. "I have rented an apartment." I heard my mother gasp.

"What are you talking about? Are you crazy?" she asked. "Lowen!" she cried as she started toward my father and me. "Talk to her. She can't do this."

My mood was mixed. On one hand, I was in charge. On the other, my mother's reaction made me wonder if I'd made a horrible mistake.

Dad took control of the escalating situation. He slowly held his hand up and said quietly, "Suzanne. Calm down."

Mom stopped, then sat back down on the couch and stared at us. Dad looked at me and said, "What's your plan?"

I tried to anticipate any questions they might have.

"I have a roommate. She's a little older than I am. She was a teacher. She works with me. You'll like her. She and her family are from here. The rent is very reasonable, it's furnished, and we can afford it together."

"When do you move in? You know what date we have to be out of here, right?"

"We move in this weekend," I said.

"Okay, then." He looked at my mother. "It will be fine." Then back at me. "Good for you." Then my parents went into their bedroom. I went into mine and began to pack.

Over the next few days, my mother did not try to change my mind, but I heard the worry in her questions. I was so young. I was inexperienced. I had no idea what it would be like to be alone, away from family. They would be across the country, and it would take days to get to me in case of emergency. I was unmoved. We'd lived continents away from family my whole life.

"Not *our* family, Nancie. *We're* your family," Mom replied.

"Mom, you were twenty when you married Dad," I reminded her. My mother looked at me and said nothing. After that we did not discuss the move.

Rosemary and I moved in on that weekend. There was not much to bring. Some books, my stereo and record albums, a few photos, and our clothes. A couple of times during the last weeks before my parents left Fort Carson, they came to drop off boxes filled with cleaning products, household items my mother couldn't take but didn't want to give up, and even a box filled with cordials and liquor. I felt very grown up, although I was more into beer than hard liquor at the time. Somehow, I translated the alcohol as their final admission that I was an adult.

My nomadic life continued after I left Colorado. I moved to Maryland, and then, over the next twenty-five years, touched down for a short while at various exits on the beltways around Baltimore and Washington, DC, with my husbands and children during and after two marriages that ended.

~

The process of moving out of the beach house and into my father's home was even more difficult than either of us anticipated. I had a lot of stuff. And I didn't want to get rid of any of it, though I knew I'd have to. I was used to the moving allowances military families received. Only so many pounds of belongings could be moved at no charge. The rest had to be stored or gotten rid of because any excess cost money. I learned to sort, ask if an item sparked joy, and toss those that did not long before the recent trend. If I didn't do it, my parents did it.

This time it was not about how much we could afford to move. It was about where we would put it all.

~

When my second marriage ended, my three girls and I moved from a large home to a townhouse about half the size. Despite garage sales, donations, the furnishing of my husband's new home, and a storage unit, the townhouse was full. When the girls left for college and their own apartments, they took things with them. Still, as Dad and I took inventory of what I had left, we knew I could not take it all.

Dad's house was full of items accumulated over the course of his fifty-six years of marriage. Even the two outbuildings were filled with overflow from the house.

During their years together, Mom purchased things in lots of three. She believed in being equitable and wanted each of her children to have one of everything she and Dad owned once they were gone. "That's a beautiful camel saddle. We'll take three."

Luckily, my brother has a piano of his own because there are only two in my Dad's house right now. And only two of the three cuckoo clocks they brought home from Germany now hang in my father's den. Dad gave Sharon the one Mom designated as mine, which is a good thing because there is no wall space left due to the ninety pieces of marquetry that adorn the den walls. I'm not sure how many German beer steins sit on the fireplace, but I'm certain the number is divisible by three.

Packing would not be a problem. I'd grown up on Dad's "pack three boxes a day" approach. I could do that. I could do more than three boxes a day, though he wasn't happy when, in typical fashion, I didn't follow the plan and packed ten boxes in one day, figuring I'd take some time off because I was so far ahead, only to fall behind schedule on my packed box quota.

Then there were the timelines. His were shorter than mine even when he thought to tell me what they were. And we can't forget the scheduling snafus. I was still working full-time during the day, which meant Dad and I had to coordinate any appointments for real estate agents, carpenters, plumbers, painters, and landscapers around my work schedule—if he told me about them in advance. Often they just showed up. Given that my work often involved crisis management, things sometimes got sticky.

I think Dad came closest to losing it over what we'd do with all my furniture and when it would finally be moved out of the house. He was trying to schedule cleaners, painters, and the installation of new carpet.

I tried my best. I threw things away. I donated to charities. I offered as much as I could to Rachel, Sharon, and Jane. They were not enthused. They had their own homes and space issues. Finally, I begged Rachel to take my dining room set and the entertainment center. I preferred to give things to my children for free rather than sell them for almost nothing. I insisted on keeping two wingback chairs, some end tables and a camelback sofa that fit nicely into Dad's large living room. Furniture that had not been given away to the girls or stored in the two sheds at Dad's house sat stacked in the middle of the beach house great room.

"Everything is out of the house," Dad said one day after returning from a meeting with the landscaper.

"Oh?"

"Yes, I gave it all to the guys working on the house. They were delighted!"

I thought about my beautiful bedroom suite, the one I'd saved for and bought with my own money, after the divorce. And every other piece of furniture in that pile representing my past. I could not believe that he would just give away my belongings without asking me first, but then, I could. It was as it has always been. If I'd handled it, he would not have had to. Relief that this phase and related tension of the move was over replaced any indignity at his having decided to give my things to strangers without asking.

With the beach house empty, I entered the next stage of my life. But I was still unsettled by the timing and the reasons for the move.

The day I left probably the last house I'd live in alone, I walked around inside and out. I locked the doors. I carried my deaf and blind cat, Devon, and my incontinent dog, Cricket, out to the car. I threw my suitcases in the trunk and took one last look, then headed home to Dad's. After dinner, I cleaned up the kitchen and went upstairs to put my things away. I felt welcomed, but it would take some time before I felt comfortable.

CHAPTER 3

~

The New Kid

I THOUGHT I'd fall into step quickly once I moved in with my father. There had always been an "order of the day" when I was growing up. We rose early, made our beds, showered, dressed, the kids ate breakfast, adults drank coffee, then everyone headed off to school or work. Most of that routine remained in place for Dad after Mom's death, although he had made a few adjustments.

He still rose early, at about six o'clock each morning, but now he came down in his pajamas, had his coffee as he watched the news, made himself some cinnamon raisin toast, and mixed Metamucil in orange juice before going upstairs to make his bed, shower, and dress. Instead of work, of course, he drove to the golf course to play eighteen holes of golf, whenever weather allowed, or to the gym to walk the track and lift weights. When he returned home, he made his own lunch.

There was no order to my day. I rose at some point, sometimes only fifteen minutes before grabbing coffee and sitting down to begin work in "my home office" in his home. I might get dressed before 5:00 P.M., but most of the time, I thought, "Why bother this late in the day?"

That wouldn't have worked when I was a kid, so I knew it wouldn't work now, at least not for the long term. I did the best I could to "snap to it," but soon it was clear that Dad had concerns.

"Did you find the shower okay?"

"If you don't want to use the bathroom near your room, feel free to use mine."

"There's shampoo in the linen closet in my bathroom along with extra toothbrushes, toothpaste, and soap in case you need any."

"How about you comb your hair and put on some lipstick? Then I'll drive you to the beach. We'll look at the ocean. It's relaxing. We can stop at Dumser's for a cone."

A bridge didn't have to fall on me. Soon I was waking up no later than 7:00 A.M., often earlier, getting dressed, making my bed, and having coffee with him each morning while he channel surfed between his favorite morning shows or what I refer to as America's outposts of ultraconservative propaganda. After listening to the talking heads criticize everything about women like me—from our value systems to how we looked and dressed rather than the principles and merit of what we believed—I couldn't help myself. Yes, I sank to their level.

"Wow, Dad! Look at that! Another white, blonde woman sandwiched between two white men on that couch. She sure is perky. But don't you think that dress is a little inappropriate?"

"It's fine. I like it." He tries not to rise to the bait. "Besides, this is show business."

"Exactly," I say snidely.

"They're going outside to talk to real people on the street," he informs me.

"I bet she'll be cold in that dress."

"You know . . . you sound an awful lot like your mother." Standing up, he looks at me.

Did I go too far?

"Here." He tosses the remote to me. "Go watch your commie show. I'm leaving anyway." My commie show was ABC's *Good Morning America*.

Our mealtimes were out of synch too. While I flipped back and forth between forgetting to eat for two days and wandering absentmindedly through the kitchen opening cabinets and the refrigerator searching for something to graze on, my father ate on a schedule. Breakfast took place sometime between 7:00 and 7:30, lunch sometime between 12:00 and 12:30 and dinner at 4:30 P.M. I thought serving dinner at 7:00 P.M. was a fair compromise, given I might eat as late as 9:00 or 10 P.M., until one night the poor man nearly fainted from hunger. We compromised. Dinner would be served no later than 5:30 P.M.

When it came to menus, I soon learned to follow one of my father's favorite rules: KISS. Keep it simple, stupid.

"How do you like your dinner, Dad?" I asked one night after throwing together a simple little quinoa salad with marinated chicken breast, dried cranberries, avocado, and feta cheese.

"It's . . . very interesting . . . uh, but tasty," he replied with the diplomacy of a State Department official while analyzing something on his fork.

"What is this?" he asked while studying a green glob of avocado covered with random quinoa grains.

"I'm glad you like it. Shall I make it again sometime?"

"No, that's okay," he said. "There is no need for you to work so hard."

I laughed and told him that my second husband would say, after trying one of my new recipes, "We should have that again," if he liked it. If he didn't, he'd just say, "Thank you."

We now stick to meat, potato or rice, and a tossed salad or vegetable combos most nights, though he likes the random Chinese, Italian, and German meals I make too. I am lucky enough to remember some of the recipes Mom and I learned while we were stationed overseas. Menu development continues to be a work in progress. And, God bless him, he's game for trying almost anything at least once. As he says, "I was in the Army. I can eat anything."

After moving into Dad's house, I looked for things to do that would help me feel as though I was pulling my weight, since it was clear he didn't really need me. Most weekdays my father played golf with the FOGs. The FOGs are a group of men Dad met at the golf club. The way he tells it, he thought there needed to be a system and organization for all the retired guys who showed up at the golf club each morning to tee off, so he did that and gave them a name. FOG stands for F-ing Old Guy. When they don't play golf, they go to breakfast. Sometimes they go to the casino where they use their points for free pizza.

Dad reserved Wednesdays for chores and personal business. He paid bills, scheduled and attended appointments with dentists and doctors, shopped, and took the trash to the local waste transfer station (county dump).

I did what came naturally. When I was not working, I took over the grocery shopping, cooked our meals, including having his lunch prepared for him when he came home from golf, did laundry, vacuumed, dusted, gardened, and, on Saturdays, I worked with him to polish any silver and brass that needed it. On Sundays, we'd go for a ride as we'd done as a family when I was a child, often grabbing lunch or dinner.

Eventually, I assimilated well enough to know what chores needed doing on what days, and adapted my work hours to fit Dad's schedule. I would fall, exhausted, out of the workweek into weekends for a little R&R. But I was still not feeling at home, and I felt far from rested or relaxed. I wanted to know I was contributing enough. I didn't talk to Dad about how I was feeling. It bothered me that I still didn't feel as though I belonged in my own father's home. Dad's reassurances did not console me.

When I apologized for not getting something done because of a crisis at work or some other reason, he would say, "Don't worry about anything. I want you to relax. The world won't end because the laundry doesn't get done."

After more than six months (the magical amount of time it had always taken for me to get used to a new locale, home, school, or job after years of moving), I still felt out of place. I panicked a little. This was not going to be a short tour. I would not be packing up again in eighteen months, leaving behind my baggage, taking only what I wanted to take with me, and starting over as I had my whole life. I was here for the duration, and I wanted to be. I knew I needed to figure out the reasons for my discomfort. It was my problem, not his, and I knew it was my responsibility to find the solution.

CHAPTER 4

~

Tea and Toast

O NE AFTERNOON after getting somewhat established at Dad's house, I wandered down the back staircase from the room where I conducted business to grab a cup of tea. "Tea at three" most afternoons had been a ritual for me since I was three or four while my mother and I lived with my father's parents during the time Dad was stationed in Korea.

As I walked away from my desk, I surveyed what had been until recently my father's "music room." Here he housed all his albums, tapes, and CDs, and the various types of equipment necessary to play them on. He even had antique gramophones. I winced a bit knowing that I'd displaced him from one of his favorite spots in the house. I knew how he loved listening to music and the enjoyment he got from fiddling with his audio equipment.

Once in the kitchen, I put the kettle on and headed to the cabinet to decide what type of tea I'd have. I heard the television on in the den. I found Dad, as usual, watching a baseball game. As I came in, he muted the sound.

"Sorry to disturb your game, Dad. I'm having a cup of tea and just wanted to know if you'd like one, too."

"That would be nice," he said. Then he added, "Your mother and I had tea every afternoon, you know."

That Mom and he had tea each day didn't surprise me. The fact that he'd shared that with me did, and I was pleased.

I told him that I loved tea breaks too.

"Your mother got me started on tea," I said, and told him how every afternoon Grandma sat down for tea at the kitchen table after a day of grocery shopping, housecleaning, taking care of her father, Pop, and me when mom wasn't there.

"After tea, that's when she'd start Grandpa's dinner." My grandfather worked the night shift as a typesetter.

"She always made me a cup of tea, too. Half tea, half milk, a lump of sugar."

Dad nodded.

"Cambridge tea, Nana called it," he said.

I told him that I knew it was also called "cambric tea" or "milk tea" by some.

"At Grandma's, there were always cookies with tea. I remember Lorna Doones, ladyfingers, and Vienna Fingers. Do you know that for years I thought that was what was meant by the term finger foods?"

We laughed and I headed back to the kitchen to get the tea ready. I offered him a selection of teas I brought with me.

"No. Lipton's is fine," he said. "Just a little half and half. No sugar."

~

From then on, "tea at three" became a shared and permanent part of the order of our days together. It started casually.

Each day I would come down, put the kettle on and go to the den to check on him.

"Tea, Dad?"

He always said, "Oh, is it that time? Yes. That would be nice."

Then I would select two mismatched mugs from the collection my parents amassed over their marriage and many moves, which

I'd found hidden in a cabinet in the kitchen. While the tea steeped (exactly three minutes), I put a few cookies on a plate before I carried it in to him.

After taking his first sip, he always said, "This is good. Thank you, hon." Then he would sit back in his recliner and seem to relax.

Our first conversations over tea were light. I asked him how he and the FOGs had fared on the fairway that morning. He asked me how things were going "at the office." Sometimes something would occur to him about my mother, his childhood, or his experience as a soldier. I not only listened, I asked questions.

One day I came down to find two porcelain mugs I didn't recognize on the counter.

"Dad, are you ready for your tea?" I asked from the kitchen.

"Yes," he said. "Did you see the mugs I put on the counter?"

He walked into the kitchen and held up one of the mugs. He pointed out that they were porcelain and he had dessert plates to go with them.

"Your mother really liked this pattern. We used to have our tea in them all the time."

"Would you like your tea in these from now on?" I asked him.

"That would be nice," he said.

While the water boiled and he waited in his den, I searched for the dessert plates. I found them in a stack, hidden behind a myriad of other teacups, saucers, and dessert plates in the dining room hutch. I pulled out two of the plates and used them for the treats that day and every afternoon after.

~

While preparing tea one afternoon, I realized that there were no treats. The week had gotten away from me and I hadn't been shopping. In a bit of a panic, I couldn't find anything sweet to accompany the tea and there was no time to bake anything that late in the day or in the fifteen minutes I allowed myself for a break on workdays. Then I thought of something my grandmother and mother made for me from time to time while I was growing up.

"Dad, we're out of cookies and cake, so I made you cinnamon toast to go with your tea. I hope that's okay."

"That's fine," he said, and we sat quietly. He smiled. "Your mother and I used to have tea and toast every afternoon after work when we were courting."

"Courting, Dad? Really?"

"Yes. Under the 15th Street Bridge."

"The 15th Street Bridge?" I was not sure what he meant.

"The Kings Highway Station in Brooklyn. There was a platform there above the station. They called it the 15th Street Bridge. We'd meet after work on Wall Street and ride back to Brooklyn on the subway. As you walked down the stairs, on the right there was a little hole-in-the-wall coffee shop. We'd order tea and split an order of toast. It was all we could afford. Then we'd both go to our own homes."

"Was it crowded after work?" I imagined the mobbed scenes of Brooklyn subways I'd seen in photos and films.

"No. Most people went straight home. Or some, like your mother's father and your Uncle Jack, would stop in at the American Inn, the bar next door to the station."

"How many tables could they fit in such a small space under the station, Dad?" I asked, my mind automatically starting to formulate a business plan for a coffee shop that could expect times during each day when the number of commuters was light and others when there was not enough space to serve a rush-hour crowd. How would turning people away have affected business?

"Oh, they had a counter. We sat there." He looked at me with a sly grin. "So we could touch knees and talk. And just look at one another."

I tried to remain expressionless. I didn't want him to stop, yet I was a bit uncomfortable thinking about my parents, goofy-eyed, in puppy love.

My father was sharing information I'd never heard. My mother had talked to me about where they met, their courtship, and their early years of marriage, but these were brief conversations, and she didn't go into much depth. She would share a little bit, then laugh. Sometimes, she'd frown, then move to some other topic.

Where my mother seemed to try hard not to romanticize their relationship, Dad did not. His version of their story and the way he told it was so loving. When Mom spoke of that time, she did not reveal how much she loved him or whether she knew how much he loved her. Her telling was almost a recitation. "We bumped into each other at the subway one morning on the way to work. We dated. We got engaged. One day he up and enlisted in the Army without telling me. The rest is history." And a painful history, I would come to realize.

I knew that my parents dated briefly during high school. They attended James Madison High School. My mother did tell me, but late in life, that early in her freshman year, she'd seen this very handsome boy in the hall wearing a hideous green letter jacket from another school.

My father laughed when I told him what she'd said. "Oh, yes. It was my Saint Brendan's jacket. And she followed me. She wanted to see where I was going."

"Where were you going?" I asked him.

"To the principal's office," he said sheepishly.

Dad said that he was a sophomore when he met Mom. He'd transferred to Madison from Brooklyn Prep, a Jesuit high school where athletics and demanding scholastics were too much for him. I was the one who told him that his oldest brother, Bill, had paid his tuition to go to Brooklyn Prep. He did not know that.

"I got no support at home. My father and mother never finished high school. There was no sense of how important education was in my home. People were always coming and going. I couldn't study in my room, at the kitchen or dining room tables. There was no one who pushed me academically. So I transferred."

After dating for a year, Mom and Dad split up. No real reason, they just drifted apart. She was busy with school and a part-time job at the public library in Sheepshead Bay. He devoted his time to playing baseball and basketball.

"Someone asked me once if I knew your mother. 'You two dated once, right?' And I told him, 'Yes, and she is the nicest girl I ever dated.' That got back to her. She liked that."

"So how did you two get back together?"

"I saw her one day at the train station. And I walked up to her and said, 'Well, hello!' We talked for a while, and I asked her if she wanted to meet me after work for some tea or coffee. She did, and there you have it."

As my father and I sat that afternoon, the steam from our cups of tea forming a bridge between us, he reminisced about Brooklyn, Mom, and the 15th Street Bridge they met under each afternoon, and I was struck not only by what I was learning, but by how his perspective had been missing from what I did know.

From then on, our afternoon tea sessions became as important as any other meal we shared together because of the emotional sustenance we took away from the topics we discussed. We shared stories the other never heard and compared notes on those we had. What my father told me on those afternoons over the course of five years lifted the veil that had shrouded who my parents had been and who they became. He would reveal so much about my own life by adding detail to stories I had been told by others or had shaped through my own childhood perceptions. These conversations illuminated both our pasts and this new stage of our relationship. Through them we began to learn how and why we wound up in this place together.

PART II

We are all of us palimpsests; we carry the past around, it comes surging up whether or not we want it . . .

—PENELOPE LIVELY, *Ammonites and Leaping Fish: A Life in Time*

CHAPTER 5

~

Mustang

T HEY CALLED men like my father *mustangs,* military slang for officers who began their service as enlisted men. Mustangs were older and more experienced than other officers of their rank since, in those days at least, most officers received commissions from one of the service academies like West Point or Annapolis. Others had progressed through the ranks from enlisted to officer after service in World War II or Korea. My father enlisted and rose through the ranks from a private to full regular Army colonel before he retired after thirty-one years.

"After I married your mother, I realized I had a family that I'd have to take care of," he told me one day.

We were having tea on the patio in the backyard and enjoying a late spring day before summer humidity set in. Dad was sitting at the patio table, under the umbrella, covered in his 100+ SPF sunscreen.

"And?" I waited patiently as I evaluated which herbs I needed to replace in the flower bed I'd tended outside the kitchen door. More basil. Always more basil. Lots of cilantro, or maybe I should stagger the cilantro plantings throughout the summer, so the heat didn't kill them all at once.

"After the weekend we eloped, I went back to post and I talked to my first sergeant, Sergeant King, and asked him what I had to do to get promoted to corporal. He just laughed at me and said, 'You wouldn't make a good corporal.' Then he asked me if my new wife could type. When I told him yes, he told me to bring her in the next Saturday. So I did, and he had her type up my application for officer candidate school."

"And the rest is history," I commented.

"I can still see your mother following his instructions and typing away. He told her exactly what to say."

I laughed, "A good man, protecting the integrity of the enlisted ranks."

Dad laughed too. "Right."

I was not familiar with this story. I'd certainly heard my mother's version of how they were engaged, with a ring he picked out without her input, certainly not the one she would have chosen; how he enlisted in the Army without telling her he was even thinking about it, and left a few days later; how she'd taken the bus from New York City to Augusta, Georgia, to break up with him. Just before I could muster the courage to ask her whether a letter might not have been just as effective, she'd said, "And then we eloped. It made my mother very sad." And from my superior perch on the tree of teenage knowledge and insight, I wanted to chirp, "If it was so bad, why did you marry him?" Wow! Sometimes, when I look back, I want to slap myself.

"Mom told me you enlisted on a Friday and shipped out the following Monday. She said you didn't tell her you were going to enlist. One evening, you just announced you had enlisted and that you were leaving in a few days."

As I weeded the flower bed and boxes that bordered the patio in the back of our house, I looked up at him. Dad looked out across the lawn to the pool from his chair under the umbrella.

"Yes. That is true."

"Seriously?" I turned to look at him.

36

"Mom said she had no clue, that you did not discuss it with her first. One day you said, 'Oh, by the way, I'm leaving for Camp Gordon, Georgia, on Monday. I enlisted. Isn't that great?'"

"I don't think I said, 'Oh, by the way. . . .' or 'Isn't that great?' But, yes, that's pretty much how it went along, with some shouting and tears."

"Don't you think you should have discussed it with her? You were engaged. It affected her too."

"Absolutely not. It was better that way. It left no time for her to get too upset and it was the best thing at the time. You didn't know your mother."

I stood up. Then I stared at him. "I didn't know my mother?"

"You didn't know her then."

For most of my life I handled conflict differently than my mother. I lived defensively. I assumed positive intent from others while I listened to the signals my gut transmitted. I anticipated every possible manner of assault, defended against all of those, and then hoped for the best. If I waved a flag, it would have been white with lettering that spelled out: "The best offense is a good defense." Mom and Dad held to "the best defense is a strong offense" concept. And in the case of Dad's enlistment, "It's easier to apologize later than to ask for permission ahead of time."

Dad explained that after graduating from high school, he had been working for Johnson & Higgins on Wall Street, first as a runner and then as an insurance underwriter. As I tried to picture my father at various stages of his life as one of the millions of people who caught trains into New York City every day, I did a quick analysis. What if he had not joined the Army? An involuntary shudder ran through me. I could not picture him in any other career. I turned my mind around and headed back to our discussion before it dove headfirst into imagining what my life would have been like had he chosen a different course and whether I'd have been born at all.

"Why in the world did you decide to join the Army then?" I asked him as though it were not a better choice than sitting behind a desk all day for forty-five years writing insurance documents. Dad raised his eyebrows.

"Because of Mr. Gerke," Dad said. He explained that on the day Mr. Gerke retired, everyone gathered around his desk to say goodbye.

"Forty years with the company and he got a flimsy cardboard box to empty forty years of desk crap into, a $75 savings bond, and a cheap gold watch. They said some nice things. Everybody clapped, and then they all left him standing there staring at the box, wondering how he'd get it home on the subway."

Dad shook his head. "Every time I hear 'Is That All There Is?' I think about that."

I refrained from saying that these days, four years with a company would be an amazing feat.

"That was the saddest thing I'd ever seen, so I walked over and asked him if he'd like to join me and your mother for a drink after work."

I imagined my father, the cheerful, optimistic, and enthusiastic young man smiling out from photographs I looked at from that time. I tried to imagine myself at the end of forty years with a company, toting a cardboard box and my cheap gold watch to a bar to have a drink with two kids in their twenties. I could not. Not even for the free drink. Not after forty years.

"He said he'd like that, so your Mom met us downstairs and we went out and had a great time. He thanked us. I was glad I'd asked him. Not one of the men he'd worked with all those years said, 'Hey, let us buy you a drink.' It was sad. I felt bad for him."

"So you decided to join the Army because you didn't want to wind up like Mr. Gerke?" I asked, trying to clarify.

"Damn right," Dad said. He thought for a while and said, "We had such a nice time that evening. You know your mother could talk to anyone and was so interested in people. Do you know he tried to put the move on your Mom?"

"Are you kidding me?" I don't know why I was surprised, but before I could ask Dad how he and Mom handled that, he went on.

"'I should have stayed in the Army,' Mr. Gerke told me, 'The best time of my life was when I was with General Pershing.'"

"Okay, you joined the Army because Mr. Gerke had a great time with General Pershing, and you thought . . ."

Dad interrupted me: "No, Nancie. Not just that. In those days, remember, there was still a draft. The Korean War was going on. It was better if you enlisted. You had more choices than if you were drafted."

I thought back to the Vietnam War. The draft was still in force then. I remembered the boys in my senior high school class weighing options, some opting to enlist for various reasons, including more choices, patriotism, or simply because their birth date was high on the draft lottery list—while others worked on acquiring deferments.

"And I wanted to get the hell away from my family. It was a way out," Dad said.

"How did Mom take the news?"

Dad laughed. "She was not happy, but we focused on the opportunities. In those days it was one of the best for men. Training, the G.I. Bill . . . and I saw the difference in the guys from the neighborhood when they came back after the war or after spending time in the service. They were mature. Focused. So I decided to enlist. And I left the following Monday."

"So you shipped off to Camp Gordon in beautiful Augusta, Georgia."

"I was off to see the world," he said.

"And the chance to see Korea."

"Yes. And that."

"You know, Dad, Mom told me that she came down to Georgia to break off the engagement. How did she get from that to married within hours of getting there?"

He looked at me and said, "I messed up." The guilt in his voice and expression was palpable.

Dad explained that he was supposed to have made reservations at the guesthouse where visiting girlfriends or family stayed.

"Things got away from me, and by the time I got over there, they were filled up.

"Your poor mother. She was exhausted. She'd been on the bus for so long, and when she found out that there wasn't a room at the guesthouse, which was chaperoned, and where she'd told her mother she'd be, she was very upset.

"I told her, 'Suzie, I'll get a room at the Richmond Hotel.' Well, that made her mad. 'I'm not staying in any hotel with you,' she said."

"Well, certainly not, Dad," I told him, "After all, how would that look, her wanting to break up with you and all?"

"I wasn't going to stay there with her," he said indignantly. "I had a bunk on post."

I waited for him to go on. By then I sat at the table across from Dad. I moved my chair out of the heat and into the shade under the umbrella and leaned forward to listen.

"That's when I came up with the plan. 'Let's just get married. Right now,' I told her. I laid out the plan. I wanted to get away from my family. She wanted to get away from hers. We loved each other. We would be fine together." He looked at me.

"What did she say?" I asked. I tried to imagine my mother, who never seemed, at least to me, to make snap decisions—she overthought everything—agreeing to this. "Never make a decision when you're tired, hungry, or upset, Nancie Laird," she used to say. This day, with my father's proposal on the table, she was about to make a snap decision.

"She just nodded her head," Dad remembered. I loved the expression on his face—a sweet smile—as he looked out toward the back boundary of the yard. Lost in thought about Augusta, Georgia, more than half a century ago.

"Then we walked over the bridge from Augusta into Aiken, South Carolina, found a justice of the peace. It was so late; they backdated the marriage license to the day before so he could marry us. We were exhausted—got a hotel room and just fell asleep."

I am not sure whether I was more moved by the story itself or how my father told it.

"Poor Mamie," Dad recalled, speaking of my mother's mother. "When she got your mother's telegram, she called the justice of the peace to make sure we were really married and on what day so that she could put a notice in the newspaper."

Knowing my grandmother, especially from my mother's stories, I knew that action was her way of assuring that if my mother got pregnant, there was documentation that she'd been married more than nine months earlier than any baby that might issue from this unfortunate situation.

"I went back to post on Monday and your mother, I couldn't believe it, went right out and got a job at Sears and found us an apartment."

"Well, as your mother used to say about Mom, 'No grass grew under Suzie's feet,'" I told him. Dad frowned a little.

"It wasn't a good idea to send her home to live with my Mom and Dad," he said.

I knew that my mother lived with his parents in the house on East 12th Street when I was born, but I didn't know all the details of why. I'd always thought it had to do with the Army or the type of assignment my father was on.

"We found out your mother was pregnant when she fainted at the bus stop one day. It was so hot in Georgia. Some people came out of their home and carried her inside. She woke up on their couch and they were caring for her. They were lovely to her.

"We let everyone know and my mother said, 'Send Suzy home. She can live with us. We'll take care of her.'

"Your mother's parents didn't have room, and your mother could not have handled what was going on in that house, not while she was pregnant. I was going to Leadership School and then Officers Candidate School so would not be as available to her if she needed me. That's why she went back to Brooklyn.

"It wasn't a good idea," he repeated, "but I didn't know then."

I knew this story too. My mother went back to live in the house on East 12th Street, unsupported by her parents who lived across town and had their own issues to deal with. She was not treated well by my father's family for many reasons. I realized while listening to my father that the two of them lived together, alone, only five months before a lifetime of career separations began and children joined what had begun as a partnership formed in a moment of necessity, and to which they remained loyal until my mother died.

CHAPTER 6

~

Temporary Quarters

I THOUGHT everyone had a permanent address, even if the home at that address belonged to someone else and not your immediate family. I knew that if someone asked where I lived—a teacher or an MP (Military Police), for instance—I should give them the address of the home where I resided at that time, either on the post or near my father's current station. Sometimes someone or a form required my permanent address— the place they called or wrote to if you were killed in the war, lost at sea, on the lam after robbing a bank, or maybe just lost—where there would be someone who knew who you were and where you might be.

Our permanent address was 1529 East 12th Street, Brooklyn, New York, until my great-grandfather died and my grandfather retired seven or eight years later and my grandparents sold the house and moved permanently to their summer home on Long Island. At that point, I felt that I'd lost my permanent address, but by then I was in high school and worried far more about other things. In those days, it was less important for people to know where I was. I dreamt of not being found.

My great-grandparents, John and Anna Marie Murphy, bought the house in Brooklyn for $4,000 in 1909, and there they raised their five children. It served as many peoples' permanent address.

It is where my paternal grandmother and grandfather, Eleanor and Charles Young, moved with my father and his two brothers when my other great-grandfather, William Joseph Young, died and the house they lived in had to be sold. It was where my great-uncle Al stayed between marriages and during a time he was ill. My grandfather's cousin Elsie West summered there between academic years while doing research at the New York City Public Library for her book on Washington Irving. And it was where my mother went to live temporarily while she was pregnant with me, and then again off and on during the first few years of her marriage to my father when he was on assignment and she could not travel with him. It was both the most wonderful experience and, as my father recalls, an unbelievably bad idea.

My mother and father considered "12th Street" an address and that's all. I saw it as my *real* home, the one I was torn away from and to which I always wanted to return. My grandparents did nothing to prevent me from thinking that. In fact, they encouraged it.

～

One afternoon, Dad and I drove through some small towns on the Chesapeake Bay side of the Eastern Shore. The places nestled on the tributaries off the Bay are rich with history and a culture all their own. I took photographs of the landscape and the old homes and soaked up the atmosphere; all of this as I looked for the setting or at least the feel of one where characters in a novel I was working on at the time would live.

Decades ago, on my first trip to the beach with the young man who would become my first husband, I remarked that I felt calm, almost immediately, once we crossed the bridge. On this day, with Dad at the wheel, I was reminded again of how much I loved the terrain—fields of summer wheat, corn, or melons, farmers cultivating rows of crops. Glimpses of deer on the edges of fields. Geese gleaning harvested fields. Later we would find that my mother's ancestors had settled an area between Oxford and Cambridge. I liked thinking that I had roots here. A new permanent address in the truest sense.

Somewhere on the road between Salisbury and Cambridge, Dad shared, "It seemed an obvious solution to me when my mother said, 'Send Suzy home. I'll take care of her.' And I believed her." He shook his head.

"It was not a good experience for Mom, was it?" I asked, though I knew. I wanted to hear specifics. Mom had spoken to me generally about the way she was treated by my grandparents during the times she stayed with them, but I wondered what she had shared with Dad.

I am blessed, and cursed, with clear childhood memories. My mother confirmed many of my early ones, so I believe I know the difference between those that really happened the way I remember them, and those that are probably a blend of those told to me and my imagination. Some say early childhood memories prove a happy childhood. I consider that, overall, I had a happy childhood. I never doubted I was loved. The doubt came later, as I hit my teenage years.

During my first few years, instinct told me that my parents and grandparents loved me and that their intentions were positive, even when the outcomes might not be. From the things that people said, I pieced together that though my father and mother hoped for the best, she was not taken care of from the time she moved into the middle bedroom upstairs to stay with my grandparents while she waited for me to be born.

~

I have very few memories of my mother inside my grandparents' home during those times we lived there while Dad was away. She would have slept in the middle room with me, but I don't remember that. She would have had to eat meals with us, but I don't remember that either. I know my mother was there, but she became invisible when we were in that house.

I remember her taking me to Prospect Park where we fed the ducks. I remember going to the zoo with her. She took me to see her parents and my Aunt Diane at their apartment, we visited her old girlfriends, we took the subway to see my other grandmother at her job at Abraham & Straus, and sometimes we saw a movie together. But in my memories, two of the three beds in the center bedroom on the second floor were empty when I slept. And my grandparents and my great-grandfather, Pop, seemed to be the only ones who ate meals with me unless there was company like my great-uncle Harry, his wife Helen, or my Uncle Jack. My mother never had tea with us in the afternoon that I remember.

When I look back, it is as though whenever I walked through those doors on East 12th Street, my mother disappeared, like a genie going back into her lamp. My father said she felt that way too.

~

My great-grandfather, Pop, slept in the third bedroom on the second floor. He and Nana gave my grandparents the front room when they and their boys moved in. He had lost his sight by the time I arrived. When I was three or so, and we walked slowly down the stairs together, I would walk behind him so I didn't trip him and so he didn't fall on me. I watched his right hand grasp the banister, the long, thin, and crooked fingers of his left hand softly touching the wall as he descended. I remember being fascinated by his hands. They were pale, the skin thin like tracing paper, his veins so blue.

"I can see through your skin, Pop," I'd say.

"Yes, you can, dear. Yes, you can. You can see well enough for both of us." And he'd laugh.

Pop was usually downstairs by the time I woke up. Every day he ate the same thing: oatmeal, a three-minute egg, some bacon, and toast. His prune juice and coffee were always in the same place, as were his pills and vitamins, just in front of the prune juice glass to the right of his plate. I loved to watch him glide his hand from the edge of the table as he reached for his vitamins. He slid it forward on the table, using his thumb to feel the plate as a guide and his index and middle finger crawling across the red-and-white checkered tablecloth toward his juice glass as he felt for the pills.

After breakfast, I'd go upstairs with Pop while my grandmother washed the dishes and cleaned the kitchen. We'd sit in his bedroom, which had a lot of light since he had a corner room. While we listened to the opening of *Don McNeill's Breakfast Club* on the radio, he piled stacks of quarters, dimes, and nickels on the side table next to the crystal bowl full of sour balls. I might march around the room as though I were part of Don McNeill's audience singing, "America awaits, the breakfast club is on the air!" as everyone sang the opening song, or I'd peer out one of the windows to see the Davis' house next door. Their house was larger, and they had a big, long yard. Mr. Davis always looked cranky, but he wasn't at all. He was just ill, my grandmother said. Sometimes he'd see me and wave. I wasn't sure if I should be watching him, so I'd wave back then go sit next to Pop.

Before I'd say goodbye to Pop to go shopping with Grandma for that day's groceries or a trip to the pharmacy on Kings Highway, he'd give me some coins so I could buy a box of Smith Brothers cough drops for myself. Sometimes he asked me to bring him a box, too. I never thought what it was like for Pop to sit alone in that room most of the time, listening to the radio; my grandmother (unless others were visiting) was his only company.

~

I looked over at my father as we drove. He was as old as my great-grandfather was during that time, and I was as old as my grandmother had been. When Dad was not playing golf, running errands, or on what I call "dad trips" with me in the car, he sat in his chair, watching television—baseball, basketball, and golf mostly—his only company (unless others are visiting) me. He seemed content. Relieved that we spent as much one-on-one time together as we did, I promised myself that it would not change. My father would not sit alone like Pop. Unless he wanted to.

"I don't have a lot of memories of Mom in that house, Dad, except when there were gatherings, like Thanksgiving or Easter."

"Probably because she tried to get out as much as she could. She didn't feel welcomed or comfortable with them. They were bastards to her. And they tried to take you over. One day she came home, and my father had rolled up the mattresses on her bed. Who knows why? That's when she got an apartment in Sheepshead Bay. She was pregnant with your brother and had to walk up three flights of stairs. It was harder once she had your brother. No one helped her. She had to rely on my parents to watch you from time to time, and every time she'd pick you up, it was a struggle to take her own child home."

I could tell Dad was still angry and sad. I was, too, hearing this. And ashamed. I remembered some of those instances where I wrapped myself around my grandmother's legs and screamed to my mother that I didn't want to go with her. She would look at me, then look at my grandmother, and say, "Alright then. You have a nice time with Grandma, Nancie. I'll be back tomorrow to pick you up."

I did not share this with Dad. It was still too sad.

"But she managed by herself until I got home from Korea. Your mom picked me up when I got back. And then, boy, did she let me have it."

"You mean Grandma didn't insist on going too?" I asked. I remembered my grandmother always picked Dad or my Uncle Bill up from the train or Patterson Field when they returned home for short visits.

"They knew I was coming in that week," he said, "but your mother and I kept the day and time a secret from them so that we could have some time alone. They always insisted on infringing. We went straight to the apartment. When I saw it and learned what had happened, I made sure your mother never stayed with my parents again."

"And I said to them when I saw them, 'By the way, thanks for taking such good care of Suzy.' They knew exactly what I meant."

"Did they?" I wondered.

"They sure did," he said with certainty.

~

I told my father the memories I'd retained from that day. I remember clearly that he came through the kitchen door, and I looked up to see him standing there. Someone asked me, "Do you know who this is?" and I replied, "That's my Daddy." I remember running to him and getting a big hug and being happy. My father confirms that really happened.

I decided to share what my grandmother told me once while she and I had tea one afternoon during a summer visit after our return from Germany. As always, she described the homecoming in grand and dramatic detail.

"I met your father and brought him home. We walked through the kitchen door. He was so handsome in his uniform and just back from Korea. There you were, as you always were, playing in the corner near the radiator and the basement door, concentrating on some game. And when you saw your father, you jumped up and ran to him. You nearly flew across the room and into his arms crying, "Daddy!"

My father was laughing at this point.

I went on, "Then she said that you said, 'They told me she wouldn't remember me.' I asked her if you cried, Dad. And she said, 'Yes, he did. Everyone cried.' Did you really cry, Dad?" I giggled.

"Oh, for Chrissake. What a bullshit artist," Dad said. I looked at him. We both started laughing again.

Until that moment I had no memory of Mom in that scene at all, but then I remembered. They came through the door together and she stopped, fading into the background behind him, as he made his entrance. Yet again, inside that house and among those people, she became invisible.

CHAPTER 7

~

New Recruit

*T*HE FIRST SEEDS of any tension between my mother and me were planted back then by my grandparents, who led me to believe she wanted to keep me away from them. These seeds germinated and grew. It was unfair, but my grandparents seemed more like parents to me than she did. If I compared ours to other families, my mother seemed more like an older sister. I believed they loved me more than she did. They never yelled at me. They seldom told me no. Discipline and punishment, if necessary, was carried out gently. Even after my brother was born, I felt I was more loved than he. I felt bad about believing my grandparents loved me more than my brother because I adored him. My grandmother told me that when we went to pick him up at the hospital on Governors Island, I said, "Give him to me, he's mine."

~

I admit now that I was not in the least bit happy to hear that my mother was going to have another baby, which only added to the conflicting feelings I had about her that my grandparents nurtured. By the time I learned what seemed to be happy news for everyone else, we were living in Brooklyn again because my father had been shipped to Korea.

"Isn't it wonderful, Nancie? Soon you'll have a little sister or brother to play with," my grandmother told me.

When I responded that I did not need or want a new brother or sister, everyone laughed at me and let me know that, unfortunately, I was not in charge of that.

"I know you'll be such a wonderful big sister. And when you see the baby you'll fall in love and want to be with it every moment," Aunt Julia told me.

I gave this a lot of thought. It seemed that no one cared what I thought about this situation. I came up with a plan. If there were to be a new baby, I wanted it to be a boy. At least then I'd still be the only girl. Apparently, my attempts to set myself up as being special began for me when I was quite young. I went into stealth mode.

When people asked me if I was happy that I'd be a big sister soon, I'd reply, "Oh, yes."

When they asked me if I wanted a baby sister or a baby brother, I'd respond, "I want a baby brother."

Each night at bedtime, my nightly prayers included, "And please send a little baby boy to be my little brother. I will love him and protect him forever."

With my brother's birth, a new family story unfolded. Though Dad had been in Korea, he filled in the parts that were missing from the versions I heard from Mom and Grandma. Mom was living in the three-floor walkup in Sheepshead Bay after the rolled-up mattress incident. When the labor pains began, Mom said she called my grandmother to drive her to the hospital, which required a ferry ride to Governors Island.

Grandma told me that Mom's labor progressed so quickly that by the time she, Aunt Julia, and Mom got to the ferry, Mom was almost ready to have the baby and the ferry was about to leave. I'm not sure why I didn't ask Grandma where I was, but I didn't.

Perhaps they left me with Mom's downstairs neighbor who had been one of Mom's best high school girlfriends.

"They were putting down the gate, and we were next in line," Grandma told me. "I told the man, 'You have to let us on the ferry,' but he said we'd have to wait for the next one. So I told him if we waited, your mother would have the baby right then and there on the ramp, and it would be his responsibility, so they squeezed us on."

Dad told me that Mom, still upset from all the events leading up to her getting her apartment, did not want my grandparents involved in my brother's birth in any way. Grandma, with her Pontiac and assignment as the family chauffeur, insisted that Mom call her. Going to the hospital in a taxi didn't make any sense.

If they almost missed the ferry, it was my mother's fault," Dad said. "Your mother called to say she needed to go to the hospital, and your grandmother didn't show up until an hour or more later. And she brought Julia. Julia didn't need to be there."

Sometimes I would go to my grandparents' home alone after my brother was born. Sometimes he would come with me.

I do remember loving him and feeling very protective of him—most of the time. I was also amazed by the differences in our bodies and his ability to shoot and hit the chandelier above my grandmother's dining room table with his "different parts" during diaper changes.

Despite visits to my grandparents from time to time, my brother and I lived at my mother's apartment. I began to love it there. The Clancy clan lived downstairs, so I had playmates. My mother took us out when she shopped for groceries, walked by Sheepshead Bay, and visited other people. We had television, and I watched *Howdy Doody, Captain Kangaroo,* and *Romper Room.* And then Dad came home.

CHAPTER 8

~

Change of Command

I KNEW I HAD A FATHER and that he was a soldier (that was reason he was away so much), but I had not quite grasped the concept of either role. At that time in my life, most children I knew had fathers who lived with them in the same house. I believed that mine did, too, in a way.

My father was blond and handsome, the youngest of the three men who grinned down at me from the silver-framed photographs of uniformed young brothers—Uncle Bill, Uncle Jack, and my father—that stood in a row on my grandparents' living room bookcase just next to the Waterford Crystal holy water bottle. I grew to love him based not only on the stories my grandmother told me, but because he was a large part of my early religious experience.

On the nights that I spent at my grandparents' home, my grandmother bathed me in an old claw-foot bathtub, which seemed to me as big as one of the boats we saw in Sheepshead Bay. Then she carried me down to the kitchen for eggnog—real eggnog, with raw eggs, creamy whole milk from the glass bottles that waited on the front step each morning, vanilla, and sugar. Grandma said the eggnog would thicken my blood and make me strong. When

53

I became full and sleepy, she carried me to the living room, took the holy water bottle and moistened the tips of the fingers of my right hand. I performed the Sign of the Cross with solemnity.

"In the name of the Father, the Son, and the Holy Ghost . . ." I would ask God to bless my father and my Uncle Bill and keep them safe.

I have no recollection of asking God to bless Uncle Jack. Maybe that was because he was no longer in the Navy. Or perhaps Grandma didn't think he needed any blessings since we saw him frequently and he seemed to be fine. I always felt bad for not asking God to watch out for Uncle Jack, but I included him with my prayers for the civilians.

Next, we'd go upstairs to say goodnight to Pop, who would say, "God bless you, dear." And I'd fling a kiss to him from the doorway. The fun part came next.

Grandma would turn on the lamp beside my bed and lift the little plastic irradiated statue of Saint Joseph holding Baby Jesus close to the lamp's bulb. I can still see her sitting on the twin bed opposite mine, long legs crossed, left arm held high inside the lampshade as she watched me, her right hand in her lap.

I kneeled on the floor, barely able to reach my folded hands to the bed, leaned my head against the mattress, and said my prayers. I had no idea what they meant. One was about our father. One was about Mary and her room of fruit. The other about four boys named Matthew, Mark, Luke, and John. Then I'd say the prayer my Uncle Jack taught me:

Now I lay me down to sleep
A bag of peanuts by my feet.
If I should die before I wake
Please give them to my brother Jake.

Grandma always laughed, then made me say it her way. She'd place Saint Joseph on the nightstand facing me. She'd draw the blackout curtains, kiss me, and say, "Sleep tight, Glory," and I, bathed in the radioactive rays of Baby Jesus and his daddy, would think about my own and wonder if he could glow green in the dark, too.

During my father's eighteen-month tour in Korea, the children of the neighborhood noticed my father's long absence.

"You don't have a daddy," they told me.

When I insisted that I did have a father, they insisted I prove it and show them who my father was. One day we marched down East 12th Street, up the front steps, through the glassed-in porch, and into the vestibule, where I rang the doorbell because I could not manage to open the big door. My grandmother answered and smiled down at the motley crew in front of her.

"They say I don't have a daddy. I want to show them."

"Be my guest," my grandmother said. She stood back and waved us through as we moved through the door. She followed us through the foyer and into the living room. She smiled, amused. This story, too, would become part of family legend. I pointed to the three pictures on the bookshelf.

"There is my Uncle Bill. He's a pilot. There is my Uncle Jack. He was in the Navy. And there is my daddy. He's a soldier."

"That's not a daddy," Eileen said, "that's a picture."

She looked at my grandmother and asked, "Where is her daddy?"

My grandmother explained, "Nancie's father is in the Army. He's away in Korea right now. The next time he is here you can meet him."

After that the children continued to tease me, adding, "Nancie's father ran away because he doesn't want to live with her."

My grandparents just laughed when I complained. "You know that's not true. You remember your father."

They were right. The soldier in the picture was not a stranger to me. I had vivid memories of the times when Mom, Dad, and I lived together when we weren't living in New York. I remembered Dad sweeping me up in the air as I tried to dart away from my mother at the swimming pool and head for the water.

"Oh, no you don't. You can't go in wearing a diaper," he'd say laughing, giving my diaper a soft swat as a reminder.

I remembered him pushing me in the stroller around the block in Fort Rucker, Alabama, on hot afternoons, patiently answering questions, never displaying boredom, but stopping at the back door each time we came around the block, where I could see my mother cooking in the kitchen. "Can we come in now?"

"No. I'm not ready," she'd say without looking up, and off we would go again until she said we could come in.

Still, to stop the taunting, I began to run to my grandfather when I saw him on the street shouting, "Hi, Daddy!" My grandparents did not discourage this and laughed; however, this could not have made my mother happy and served as another device for removing her from the picture.

When my father came home from Korea, my grandmother claimed I took him right outside and marched him up and down the block, introducing him to anyone we met.

With him holding my hand, I introduced him: "This is my daddy."

"Oh, that never happened," my father tells me. I may not have, at least not the way my grandmother described it, but I do remember walking with my father to St. Brendan's or around the corner to the drugstore on Coney Island Avenue where someone would ask, "Who's that, Nancie?" I was very happy to announce, "This is my daddy."

⁓

Dad and I were on our way to the dump in his thirty-year-old truck. As we did when we drank tea, we told stories when he drove me anywhere.

"When I learned how they treated your mother while I was away, I knew that we were on our own. We couldn't count on anyone except ourselves. We had to be our own little unit. We wouldn't ask them for anything again. From then on it was just your mom, me, and you kids. We finally came into our own when we moved to Germany."

"It took an ocean and a new continent to escape those people," I said, and laughed.

To me, our life as a family began when Dad moved into the apartment while he arranged for our move from Brooklyn to Fort Sill, Oklahoma.

My mother was so happy. Dad played with us and fixed things in the apartment. I had no idea that I would not see either set of grandparents frequently or how far away this place Oklahoma was. I had a father, a mother, a baby brother, and a whole new lifestyle. The era of packing up, moving out, and discovering new places together had begun. The platoon was on the move.

CHAPTER 9

∾

Maneuvers

CROSS COUNTRY TRAVEL was quite different in 1955 than it is today, especially by automobile. Most of the roads we traveled on were single lane since the Federal Highway Act was not signed into law until 1956. There were no charge cards either. Dad kept all the money they had to their name in his pocket, and they budgeted carefully. The processes we'd follow for all our road trips from post to post began then. After eight to ten hours on the road, Dad would pull up to a hotel and my mother would run in, then come out to announce whether we'd stay or drive on. When she'd announce, "They want too much money," Dad would say, "Okay. Let's move on." After two or three tries, we'd find a place that fit the budget.

Unless we were on a turnpike or "major road," there weren't any restaurants along the way. Mom made sandwiches in the car and gave us fruit; we'd take advantage of restaurants that were open if we happened to drive through a town at the right time. We also ate in people's homes.

"You'd see a sign that said, 'We Serve,' lunch or dinner." Dad told me. "They usually had two or three selections. Almost always mashed potatoes." He smiled. My father loves mashed potatoes. "They were nice people, and we enjoyed talking to them."

I was introduced to Howard Johnson restaurants and hotels on that trip. Dad gave me a taste of my first clam roll. Thereafter, clam rolls were my favorite food on road trips. My brother would get the kid's hotdog meal and I'd ask for a clam roll with coleslaw on the side and a scoop of pistachio ice cream for dessert.

"When we got to Tulsa, we stayed in the Thunderbird Hotel," Dad remembered. "At least, I think that was the name. And we ordered breakfast from room service. That was high living for us."

I didn't remember that part of our trip, but I remembered the Magic Fingers massaging beds and that sometimes you had to put money in the television to watch it.

"Remember having to go into the woods to pee? Or using the little pot from our potty chair?" I asked Dad.

"Well, you do what you have to do," he said.

I learned a lot about teamwork on our trips. Things went better if people tried to get along, if we were considerate with one another, if my brother stayed on his side of the backseat. There were no seat belts then either. My brother and I took turns riding in the back window, sometimes napping, sometimes watching the people in the car behind us. I remember being small enough to stand up straight in the back seat or run from one side of the car to the other until one of my parents yelled, "Sit down!" There were a few bloody lips along the way when Dad stopped short and one of us flew into the other or into the backs of Dad's or Mom's seat.

Once we arrived in Lawton, Oklahoma, we moved into quarters on Fort Sill. There were two bedrooms, one bath, and lots of speckled black linoleum that seemed to go on forever because we had no furniture. Dad and Mom bought some furniture at Sears, including a loveseat, chair, and coffee table, but within a year Mom found a furnished duplex off post in downtown Lawton. We lived there for the rest of our time in Oklahoma. I saw my first buffalo, jackrabbits, snakes, and oil wells.

We lived through a tornado that pelted our neighbors' storm cellar doors with hail the size of softballs. I learned that people could live underground if they had enough food, water, and air. I was introduced to the histories of the Comanche and the

Anadarko. Pictures of me at the time show me wearing a cow-girl outfit, a six-shooter, and a feathered headband, innocent and unaware of the tragic history of Native Americans in this country.

My brother and I were happy. Mom and Dad seemed happy too. Sometimes late on a summer afternoon, Mom would pile Little Lowen (that's what we called my brother Jim then) and me into the car. We'd meet Dad and drive to a picnic area and eat baked potatoes out of "tin foil boats" before Dad drove us to the officers' club swimming pool or we went home because he was that day's Duty Officer. I loved the nights they'd dress us in our paja-mas and take us to the drive-in movie. Dad pulled up to a pole in the ground, rolled the window up or down to the right level, and hung the speaker so we could all hear. My parents allowed us to watch the coming attractions and the cartoons before the featured film, but then we were tucked into the back seat and expected to fall asleep. I seldom did until we rode home.

Instead, I saw movies like *Friendly Persuasion* and *High Noon* by peeking over the seat. I tried not to make any noise and moved slowly to avoid their attention. I thought I fooled them until we got home, and I waited for my father to pick me up to bring me into the house.

"I'll carry your brother in, Nancie. Since you're awake, you can make it in yourself." Sometimes he'd wink at me, sharing my secret.

After nearly two years, Dad was transferred to Fort Benning, Georgia, for a short assignment before heading to Germany. That is when military posts began to feel like home to me. Though they were not exactly alike, you could expect certain things—a post exchange, commissary, dispensary/hospital, NCO (non-commis-sioned officer) and officers' clubs, barracks, motor pools, chapels, and parade fields. No matter how different the last town or city we lived near was from the one we moved to, driving onto the post felt like coming home. Everything was familiar, from the military vehicles to the color of the buildings to the sounds.

We could expect to hear "Reveille" in the morning when the flag was raised, "Retreat" in the afternoon when the flag came down, and "Taps" at night for lights out. I loved that time of day when the trumpet would sound "Retreat" and no matter where you were—playing ball, on a swing, coming out of a building— everyone stopped as the flag came down, even if you couldn't see it. But even now, my favorite sound on any post is the sound of a platoon of soldiers marching or jogging in formation while some- one calls cadence. Whether it's the thump, thump, thump of their combat boots or the call-and-response of the cadence, I'm not sure. But it's steady and familiar. I used to think my "strut song" should be a cadence call. I seldom knew the words of the cadence being called, but I knew the "chorus":

Sound off, one two,
Sound off, three four,
Sound off, one, two—three four!

Whatever my emotion at the time—anxiety, fear, loneliness— my heart would fall into rhythm with the sound of boots hitting the asphalt, and I'd steady out. I was home.

CHAPTER 10

~

Platoon

A PLATOON IS DEFINED as the smallest unit in the United States Army, if you don't count the squads within it. To my childish mind, military families were like platoons. I felt a kinship with the young soldiers who sat among us at Saturday morning movies, shopped at the PX (Post Exchange), or worshiped alongside us at religious services on the weekends. The children of soldiers, airmen, sailors, and marines, especially when I grew up, were well versed in all things military. And this was reinforced by our parents.

While we grew up, Dad always spoke of us as a team, a team in which each of us played a part, and, he stressed, "At the end, we only have each other. The five of us. That's all. We take care of each other."

It was true that each of us had a specific role, even the children. As oldest child, though, I outranked my brothers, who shared the rank equivalent to privates, due to *years-in-grade* or, in this case, birth order.

Rank has its privilege. Seats in the car were assigned by rank. Mom sat up front with Dad. In the back seat, my youngest brother,

Clint, sat between our brother Jim and me. Jim and I got the window seats because we outranked Clint. I got my choice of window because I outranked Jim. Even now, especially since Mom is no longer with us, if my brothers and I get into Dad's car, he drives, and my brothers' first instinct is to stand back and allow me to ride shotgun, the seat my mother always occupied. I wish it were due to respect and deference, but it's just muscle memory from our basic training.

The Army's version of a platoon is led by a junior officer, usually a lieutenant supported by the platoon sergeant. Each squad has a leader. I admit to being somewhat confused about which of my parents held the highest rank in our platoon. If Dad was home, Mom might say, "You'll have to ask your father about that." And sometimes when I asked him something, he would say, "That's up to your mother." With parents, it seemed that area of expertise determined who was in charge.

Eventually, I got a sense that the ultimate decision maker had less to do with rank and more to do with a division of labor they'd drawn up together. Of course, when Dad was on TDY (temporary duty) or on a hardship tour, usually twelve months or more (Korea or Vietnam, for instance), Mom outranked everyone. No questions asked.

The summer before I turned twelve, expectations and responsibilities changed for me. My mother required surgery, and during the weeks leading up to the operation, she taught me how to do laundry, iron, and plan and prepare meals, as well as clean up afterwards, all of which I would have to do for the six weeks after she was released from the hospital. I already knew how to make beds, clean bathrooms, mop floors, vacuum, dust, and polish silver, brass, and the furniture. We all did, as these were chores we completed as a family every Saturday when we "policed the area."

I took on my new responsibilities with energy and enthusiasm. Years later my mother said she had been worried about how much I seemed to enjoy those tasks. What I really enjoyed was how much she and Dad seemed to appreciate my hard work.

There were only two real failures that I recall. I once starched dad's boxers. He let me know, "That won't be necessary. Ever again. Leave that step out." And Mom stopped me from serving hotdogs wrapped in semi-raw bacon to my brothers, my mock rumaki recipe (sans chicken liver and water chestnut slices, neither of which I'd ever seen at that point in my life) I'd cut out of *Good Housekeeping* or *The Ladies Home Journal*.

From then on, I continued to help Mom with housekeeping, while Dad taught the boys as they got older how to rake leaves, mow the lawn, and fix things around the house. But we continued to share Saturday area policing as a family.

The division of labor was clear. Inside work was women's work. Outside work was men's work. And I noticed that more and more I became my mother's responsibility, while my brothers were my father's.

~

That summer brought more changes. One day Mom called to me while I played baseball in the sandlot across from the house as I'd done for the past two summers. I was proud of my ability to play baseball as well as if not better than the boys I played with. It was the one thing I still felt totally comfortable doing. I loved the slap of the ball hitting my mitt if I squatted behind home plate or caught a line drive, loved the feeling of diving for the ball and spinning to throw it to someone else's waiting glove. And I loved hitting the ball.

She and Dad sat me down in the living room and she said, "You can't keep playing baseball with those boys."

"Why?" I asked. I looked at my father. This couldn't be his idea. He knew I was as good at fielding, hitting, and double plays as the guys. He knew how important baseball was. He'd taught my brothers and me how to play. We all played together.

"You could be hurt, Nancie."

"How?" I pointed out that anyone could be hurt, my brothers included. I always kept my eye on the ball and I never put my glove up in front of my face unless totally necessary—and then did not move it until the ball was no longer in play. I didn't stand too close to anyone with a bat. Once when younger, a boy whacked me with a bat because neither of us was paying attention. It was the last time I made that mistake. I really did not understand why we were having this conversation.

There had only been that one time the other day while pitching, when Frank surprised me by hitting a line drive that I caught in my solar plexus. It knocked me down and I lost my breath. The boys all ran to gather around me, help me up, brush the red dirt off my shirt and pants. I did not mention how much I'd liked that.

"Nancie, those boys are much bigger than you are. And they'll continue to be," Mom said. "It's dangerous, honey."

My father stepped in to help my mother. "You're a pretty girl, Nancie. What if you get hit in the face? What if you get hit in the chest?"

My mother and I stared at him. I had no idea what he was talking about. I caught my mother's expression as she looked at him too. Did she roll her eyes? Then she said, "Thank you, Lowen, I'll handle this." My father seemed relieved that he'd been dismissed.

Mom became, as she seemed always to be after that time, the messenger bearing bad news. "That's it. No more baseball. I'm sorry." Her tone reminded me that she didn't have to supply a reason, answer my questions, or entertain any appeals. The meeting was over. I hung up my glove.

In the ensuing weeks, I sulked and felt sorry for myself. I stayed in my room, sometimes watching the guys play ball without me. My parents ignored me. Then one day my mother took me to shop for clothes.

"If she thinks she's going to bribe me with clothes, she's wrong," I thought, crossing my arms and pouting in the front seat of the car. I could have cared less about clothes, or so I told myself. I soon realized our trips to the store for new clothes were for more than back-to-school garb. She bought me new gloves and hats, which I usually got only for Easter. Then a garter belt and stockings. I wouldn't be wearing those to school, I swore to myself.

A few days later she said, "Let's have tea. We'll use the silver service."

My mother gave me lessons in pouring tea and coffee using the prized silver tea and coffee service they'd purchased in Germany. I learned how to hold a cup and saucer properly, and I became proficient at how to politely ask guests their preference. My ability to field a grounder transferred to pouring scalding liquid into a porcelain cup without shaking or spilling a drop while I asked, "Cream? Sugar? One lump or two?"

One Saturday morning toward the end of summer, Mom had me dress up in a lovely coral-colored dress with white piping. I wore my white gloves, garter belt, and stockings. No hat that day. Dad took a picture of us sitting on the sofa in which Mom looks somewhat apprehensive. My expression is that of one being kidnapped, albeit by someone I knew. My eyes ask, "Why am I dressed like this? Where is she taking me? Why are we taking pictures?"

Mom and I drove to the officers' club at Fort Gordon. There we joined the other officers' wives and their daughters for the Back to School Tea. I would learn later that Coffees were held in the mornings, Teas in the afternoon. I looked around the large room. The other girls were my age or older, all in gloves and stockings, some as uncomfortable as me and others flitting about as though they'd discovered their natural calling. We took turns pouring. The room echoed with "Tea? Coffee? One lump or two?"

～

I know now that the distance between my father and me began to lengthen then, and I started to assign reasons why. He was promoted, which brought more job responsibility as well as frequent social obligations for my parents. I blamed lack of time. And I blamed my mother. I believed she was trying to prevent me from being close to my father. In addition, we readied for another move, this time to Taiwan.

I was changing, too. I had new interests, including boys, clothes, teen magazines, and the local radio station. Of course, the typical emotional ups and downs of relationships with my friends distracted me. Something else happened, too.

My mother became my primary mentor—or, as I saw it, "handler." More and more I viewed her as messenger of bad news, whether from my parents or the world at large. My girlfriends and I discussed how our fathers were "brought in" for serious discussions when "she" (our mothers) needed backup. We saw this as a demonstration of weakness rather than one of strategy and strength. So our changing relationships with our fathers seemed perfectly normal. Our delight at growing up masked our sadness about the childhood we left behind or any uneasiness we might possibly have about what the future held.

CHAPTER 11

~

Distaff

MY FATHER AND I stared at the moving boxes stacked in the back of his SUV after one of our trips between the two houses, much of the contents of which had been given to me by my parents at various stages of our lives. When I moved into my first apartment, married for the first time, and any time after that when my parents moved up to when they retired, I was a convenient and willing storage option. Some of the boxes had not been unpacked in years. I'd just carried them with me from marriage to marriage and now back to Dad's house.

Between what he and I owned and all the boxes, we could open a formal catering business. Pots and pans, multiple sets of day-to-day and formal china—all from different places and used for different purposes. One didn't get rid of such things. Who knew whether any or all of your belongings might get from one station to another during a move? And who knew what your children might need someday? Or your grandchildren?

"Why do you have all of this?" he asked me. "Do you really need it all? We could take some to the Salvation Army."

"Ha!" I laughed. "A lot of this stuff is Mom's and yours. Things you two didn't really want to get rid of yourselves. Think of them as back home where they belong. We can put what isn't needed in the shed. Maybe one of my girls will need something."

"Well, you'll sort it out," he said, and headed into the house.

"I'm taking a break first. I'll make tea."

As the water boiled, I stared at the side of the refrigerator. Random magnets supported the business cards of plumbers, electricians, and pest control companies. Pieces of notepaper listed names and numbers for doctors, the dentist, and emergency contacts.

~

Growing up, one always found the roster near the phone. This consisted of many pages of what we, today, might consider too much information about the men and women serving in my father's command at the time. Issued by the battalion, the roster contained information about the personnel assigned to it, such as name, rank, position, phone number, and home address. The column that interested me most was entitled "distaff." Here one also found the information about spouses—always female in those days as women would not be integrated into combat units until 1978—along with their children's names and ages. I used to absorb and memorize the information on the roster.

Upon receipt of a new roster, which occurred whenever Dad was reassigned or whenever one was revised to reflect changes in personnel, I looked to see if there was anyone I already knew from another assignment or who might have children my age—especially boys, once I was a teenager.

The roster was indispensable when it came to meeting people for the first time. My roster studies helped me feel comfortable, as though I already knew them, and I felt less shy. "It's nice to meet you, Mrs. Smith, and how are your three children, Shirley (female, ten), Peg (female, nine), and John (male, three)?" It helped to know whether the officer I was speaking to reported to my father, shared the same level of rank, or was the commanding officer, though my mother assured us that we were expected to behave and treat people well and with respect no matter who they were, where they were from, or what rank they held. Mom's view was that God gave us value while the army only assigned rank. God outranked the Army.

"What's distaff mean?" I once asked my father. What I really wanted to know was why that word rather than wife or family?

"Distaff—the distaff side is the spouse, these days sometimes a husband. It's the family side of things," he said. When I was growing up, though I might see a female lieutenant listed she was seldom married. I do not ever remember a male appearing under the distaff column.

I understood the separation between the military personnel and the distaff sides of the roster. But why that word? Why not "other information" or "family" instead of "distaff"?

I learned the etymology of the word distaff during my college English classes where I found that Chaucer, Shakespeare, and others used it in the works assigned to us. It related to "women's work," both at home and in the community.

They say when you marry a military person, you enlist as well, and your children are born enlisted. Though unpaid, my mother and her counterparts had jobs and expectations to meet outside the home. A military wife's level of engagement as well as whether she met the expectations imposed on her could affect her husband's promotion potential. Military wives served as members on committees and boards of the many community support organizations for soldiers and their families. In addition, Mom was expected to attend coffees, brunches, luncheons, and teas, as well as the "command performance" receptions, military balls, and other social events with my father.

"Your poor mother. We had to attend the Infantry Ball when we arrived at Fort Sill," Dad said, "and she didn't have a ball gown. We had no money. The officers wore their dress uniforms."

"What did she do?" I asked, expecting that he'd gone alone and gave sick children as an explanation for her absence.

"She told the other women," he answered. "One of them wrote home to her sister and had her send out some dresses. Your mother wore one of those. And she was beautiful."

"That's amazing"

Dad started laughing and said, "When we moved to the furnished duplex in downtown Lawton, your mother threw a Tea. We had nothing, but her friend sold silver and let her use her samples. I've never seen so much silver in my life.

"They all had to know that this wasn't your mother's silver, but one of them, she was a real bitch, said, 'Oh, Suzy, can I borrow some of this for my Tea? It's lovely.' Before your mother could say anything, her friend who owned the silver said, 'I'll help you take it over, Suzy, since I have a car.'"

Dad gave his impression of my mother's smug smile. He loves telling me about times that Mom fared well in situations where people tried to make her feel bad or hurt her.

"Your mother was such a sweet young woman. People were always trying to take advantage of her." I thought about Mom and though people may have tried, the woman I knew never seemed bothered by what other people said or did to hurt her. At least she never talked about it with me.

~

As we enjoyed our tea and I avoided dealing with the moving boxes still loaded in the back of car, Dad and I talked more about our time in Lawton. There were so many stories. Once my mother got up in the middle of the night and walked into the bathroom door, which never closed all the way without being forced. Someone had left it open. The gash on her forehead required stitches and Dad had to take her out to the post hospital.

"Imagine my surprise when I saw your mother wearing my boxers under her nightgown," he laughed, "and she'd used my lieutenant's bars as a pin because the waist was too big. I could fit my hands around your mother's waist she was so tiny."

Listening to my father's stories and sharing mine—whether we were in the car or talking over tea—reminded me of working on a puzzle with someone else. To take in the puzzle's big picture, you must dig through all the puzzle pieces. Sometimes the piece you need sits all alone on the table, away from the pile of other pieces and easy to see if you take the time to look. Sometimes you must sort through the pile to see what fits. At other times you must ask the other person if he's holding the piece that fits the space you're trying to fill. He looks at the section you're working on and hands you a piece he thinks may work. Sometimes it does and sometimes it doesn't, even when you turn it around and try it different ways. Sometimes you can finish the puzzle in one sitting, and other times it takes a summer of sitting with it, stealing a little time here, a little time there, to fiddle with it until you get it right.

PART III

Probably there is nothing in human nature more resonant with charges than the flow of energy between two biologically alike bodies, one of which has lain in amniotic bliss inside the other, one of which has labored to give birth to the other. The materials are here for the deepest mutuality and the most painful estrangement.

—ADRIENNE RICH, *of Woman Born:*
Motherhood as Experience and Institution

CHAPTER 12

~

Dissension in the Ranks

URING OUR FIRST YEAR of living together again, Dad and I laughed a lot, not only about funny memories we shared, but about new experiences as we got to know each other again. As he always had, he tried to joke me out of taking life too seriously, especially my work.

At that time, I worked as a program director for a company that runs a State Department-sanctioned cultural exchange program. About three or four times a year, I was "on call" for a week at a time in case of emergencies. This amused my father who has, for my entire adult life, asked me, "What is it you do again?" It seemed to me that he could only picture me as a secretary, a teacher, a nurse, or a wife—any position outside of those roles was either not worth remembering or difficult to wrap his brain around.

During one monthly visit to Sam's Club, the answering service contacted me with an emergency just as we were rolling our full basket to the checkout lane. Since Dad always insists on unloading the basket by himself, because I'm obviously unable to lift a head of lettuce without assistance, I walked away and found an empty aisle so I could take the call. By the time I got back, Dad was paying the cashier and she turned to look at me.

"Thank you for all you do," she said smiling.

Dad was smiling, too, so I figured something was up. I've learned to just play along.

"Uh . . . why thank you. Same to you," I responded humbly.

As we moved away Dad smiled. Then he began to laugh.

"What's going on?" I asked him.

He explained that the cashier asked him if he did all the shopping by himself.

"I told her no. I said you picked everything out and I pushed the cart." He said. "Then she asked me where you were. "I told her you had to take an important call because you are the person on duty this weekend. She asked me if you were a doctor." Dad described how he leaned in and said in a whisper, "No. State Department. She had to take an important call. She's the person on duty this weekend."

When she asked Dad if the call was important, he told her, "You know the State Department. Embassies. Wars. Who knows what it is this time?"

"Dad," I said, horrified, "I do not work for the State Department. I work for a company that runs a sanctioned program."

He dismissed me. "*I* know that, but *she* doesn't."

"I think it's illegal to represent yourself as working for the State Department when you don't."

"Oh, it may be illegal for you to do it, but I'm in my eighties. I can say whatever I want. No one takes me seriously. I'll tell them I don't know any better. Or that I don't remember saying anything like that."

"Okay, Dad. I see."

"Come on," he said. "It made her day. And mine."

"That's right. That's what I'm here for. Make fun of me. I can take it. But I wonder where my real father is."

"I'm right here, babe. Right here," he said.

A sense of humor is a wonderful thing, but if it were a martial art, my family members and I would have black belts. We wield humor like a weapon—sharp-edged when angry, self-deprecating when embarrassed or vulnerable, and as a diversion to ward off strong emotions or tears, whether our own or someone else's. It is also a useful tool for avoiding or postponing tough conversations, so despite our easy back-and-forth most of the time, when I ran into obstacles in this new territory I lived in, I still found it hard to talk to him about things that bothered me as they happened.

Some days I wondered what he was thinking. On others I knew exactly what ran through his mind but saw a familiar look in his eyes and set of his jaw, which I took to mean that discussion was not going to take place. He would keep those thoughts to himself. So I'd wait for him to say, "Listen, I want to talk to you."

∽

My mother never hid what she was thinking. If she was upset (the only word that can describe a panoply of emotions exhibited by my mother when she was unhappy), everyone knew it. She might give everyone the silent treatment for a day or two. She might get angry and bang things around as though to make sure we noticed. There were times she screamed at us and said hurtful things. One day she'd been silent first, then began to slam the cabinet doors in the kitchen and rattle the pots on the stove. I hid in my room.

Later she told me she had been counting on something that didn't happen and when it didn't, she was angry and disappointed.

"I thought you were mad at me," I said.

"Why would you think that?" she asked.

"I don't know. Just because," I replied.

"Did it occur to you to ask me? You might have asked if I was upset about something."

I wondered why she just didn't tell me. I would never ask. I was always afraid of her answer. I know now that I was not afraid of her anger at me. I was afraid that if she told me she was sad, unhappy, disappointed, or angry that I couldn't make it better. I might make even make things worse.

When I was an adult, my mother and I were sitting at the table in my kitchen while my daughters ran in and out of the room.

"Nancie," she said, "when you were growing up and I was in a bad mood or sad, why didn't you ask me what was wrong? You'd come in from school, look at me, and leave the room. Your brother always asked, 'What's wrong, Mom?' You ignored me."

I thought back to that time. I was a senior in high school. Dad had gone off to Nebraska as a bootstrapper to finish his degree. He'd only been home from Vietnam a year. As a grown woman, with children of my own, one of whom was a teenager, I had a much better sense of what she went through then—left alone again in a new place with three kids, with another move on the horizon. At the time I was just hoping and praying to finish out my senior year in the same high school.

"Mom, I don't remember it that way."

"Oh? The memory is crystal clear to me, Nancie. You would walk in, say hello, and immediately leave the room. Your brother would say, 'What's wrong, Mom?' He was sensitive."

I started to laugh. "Mom, when I walked in, I always knew if you were upset. So you're right. I'd say hello, and then look around to see if there was something I could do to help, like clean the kitchen or fix dinner, clean up my room. . .."

I told her that my recollection was that my brother would look at her and sigh before saying, "What's wrong *now*, Mom?"

"If I had said that you would have erupted. But when he'd ask, you'd say, 'Oh nothing.'"

Then Mom started to laugh. I joined her and we laughed together until we cried. It was a moment of recognition. The two of us would hold on to something and gnaw on it for decades, unable to toss it out until we worked it out.

"You're right! Now I remember," she said. "Why didn't you ever say anything?"

"Mom, it's almost twenty-five years later. Why did you not ask me then why I seemed not to care?"

"I don't know. Maybe I was afraid you didn't."

With a little insight too late, I said, "Mom, it wasn't just you. I didn't ask enough questions growing up. I was afraid too."

My mother reached over and touched my hand. "I know," she said, and smiled.

~

Yet on this new journey with Dad, I opted as I always had with him for the more familiar path of least resistance. I avoided difficult subjects, kept those things that bothered me to myself, prayed for patience on both our parts, tried not to upset or disrupt the routine, and wished for peace. In order to navigate any minefields that might appear, I looked for ways to lighten the mood or at least not make things worse, despite awareness that unspoken thoughts and feelings seeded in unresolved issues lie like dry tinder, awaiting victims to random sparks.

I've stockpiled tinder my whole life. Sometimes, probably too often, I've struck the spark that ignited the fires. I fear an apocalyptic firestorm and the direct and collateral damage that might occur if I can't control it once started.

~

A few days after I moved in with Dad, just before his real estate agent began to show the beach house to interested buyers, we drove back out to the beach house to look at a leaky outside faucet. It had been fixed once but after the winter it had never worked properly and continued to leak. I was concerned that if it leaked under the crawlspace that it could be an issue during a buyer's inspection. My father thought I was overthinking, but to humor me, he went along for the ride.

Dad looked through the opening and into the crawlspace.

"I'm going to have to climb inside. I can't get a good view from here."

"No, Dad, let's call a plumber. You can't crawl under the house."

"It's fine," he said as he began to crawl in headfirst. He looked like he'd get stuck. How would I get him out?

"Dad! No. I'm calling a plumber. You're eighty years old. What if you get stuck in there?"

"Nancie." He turned and looked at me. "Shut up."

I gasped. We stared at one another for a nanosecond; I'm not sure who moved first before I turned around and walked back to the car. I thought how ridiculous I must look, like an angry fifteen-year-old admonished by her father, fists clenched and stiff-legging it back to the car. I was sixty years old. Besides, I was stuck there. The car was locked, and he had the keys.

"No one tells me to shut up," I muttered under my breath.

I was enraged. I turned back and stomped toward the house arriving just as he disappeared through the crawlspace opening, I said calmly, firmly, and with all the respect I could muster despite the tightness in my chest, my racing heart, and lump beginning to form in my throat. I would not cry.

"Don't *ever* tell me to shut up, Dad. Please." I said.

Dad did not respond. I don't know whether he heard me or if he ignored it, but when he crawled back out of the hole, he brushed off his pants and smiled.

"All set! Let's go get some lunch."

I didn't ask if he'd heard me. As far as he was concerned, it was over, if he'd noticed it at all. As far as I was concerned, the matter was not closed. But I wasn't prepared to bring it up now. If it happened again, I'd say something.

I rationalized as we drove to the restaurant. He didn't mean it. It was just reflex. My brothers wouldn't be bothered if he said that to them. Why should I care? Besides, it wasn't the way he spoke to me all the time. In fact, hardly ever. Except in moments of anger or frustration he didn't speak to anyone that way. Then I thought of my mother's reaction if he ever said that to her. And . . . I laughed. He would never have said that to her!

For weeks afterward I rolled the moment around in my mouth like a bitter taste and realized that it was not what he'd said that upset me. It was that I had not spoken to Dad and addressed it immediately. It could have been resolved then. I hadn't followed through.

I was bothered by the "why." After all these years, why was I was afraid of his reaction? He might say, "Okay, Nancie," and dismiss me as though my reaction was an overreaction—silly, unwarranted, over-the-top, emotional, or all the above. I explored whether I *had* made something out of nothing. Ruminating over this one small piece of a whole life left me emotionally drained. I left it alone for a while but began to pay attention to what he said, when he said it, and opportunities to address issues that arose in the moment if necessary.

Within the next twelve months, Dad became ill and I was worried about him. For a week I nudged him to make an appointment with his doctor. He refused and said, "I'm fine. It's a cold. I know when I'm really sick and when I'm not."

When he wasn't better after ten days, I told him he was foolish not to at least call the doctor's office to see what they suggested, and he responded, "Nancie. Shut up."

Oh no! I thought to myself. *He's not going to get away with it this time.*

I looked at the back of his head as he sat in his recliner, but I just couldn't bring myself to speak to him about it then. He was sick. I wasn't going to argue with a sick man. Instead, I said, "Okay, Dad. I'll stop bothering you about this. We can talk about it later. I'm just worried about you."

I'd made a commitment to myself to address this with Dad, so for the next week I thought about best times to bring it up as well as what I should say. One afternoon, when he was feeling better and after we returned from a wonderful drive to Assateague Island National Seashore, I found him watching television while he played the "fake slot machines" on his iPad.

"Dad, may I talk to you about something?"

"Of course," he said as I sat on the couch and leaned forward.

"Would you please not tell me to shut up? I don't know what it is about that phrase, but it upsets me. I will stop if you say 'hush' or 'please stop' or 'that's enough' or 'I've told you how I feel and I don't want to discuss it any further,' but I cannot handle 'shut up.' It makes me feel like a child. And most of all I feel disrespected. You are the one who taught me no one should tell me to shut up. I mean, if I had told you any of my boyfriends or husbands had told me to shut up . . ."

He looked at me, "Oh. Okay. I'm sorry."

That was it. And since then, rather than "shut up" he has used different ways to tell me to back off.

"That's enough, Nancie, I heard you."

"Nancie. Okay. I get the message."

"Nancie, not now."

Sometimes he just stops and looks at me with an expression that reminds me far too much of my own when I don't want to listen to someone. These glimpses of myself made me decide that it was only fair that I start thinking more about the things I said to him as well. I asked myself when he was most likely to want me to be quiet or to give him time.

It was easy to see the pattern. If it was about his health, what he's eating or drinking, or when I thought he needed to see the doctor he resisted me. It happened when I was trying to take care of him. He was not ready for that.

~

I am sure that Dad, like me, expected times that we would hit patches of rough terrain, bumpy albeit not impassable. I noticed that when we discovered ourselves in a difficult stretch it tended to be related to incorrect assumptions or a lack of information. If we relied on what we thought we knew about each other we got stuck, tires spinning.

I soon realized that despite a lifelong belief that my father and I had a close relationship, we did not. How could we? This did not mean that we didn't love one another, that we didn't enjoy a lot of the same things or share many of the same values and our sense of humor. We just really did not know each other well at all.

This resulted in huge gaps in my base of knowledge about him and he seemed genuinely puzzled by me. I believe we were both confused about how this could happen in such a close and caring family.

Once during one of our Sunday drives, Dad and I made a list of all his assignments from the time he enlisted in the Army. We calculated that from my birth until I was eighteen, we had lived apart fifty percent of the time. Despite what we knew about one another and the experiences we'd shared while living together, there was a great deal we didn't know about what life had been like for each of us during times we'd lived apart.

When Dad was away, the role of intermediary and reporter fell to my Mother. She and Dad wrote letters or spoke on the phone if possible. While he was in Vietnam, they stayed connected through once-a-month ham radio calls and little reels of tape, recorded, and played back on tiny tape recorders. Time was limited on calls. There is only so much you can put in a letter and who knew who the ham operator was or if the tapes might fall into the wrong hands. Depending on where Dad was and what was going on, there had to have been things she either forgot or chose not to tell him. Unlike today's military men and women who can communicate through video chat on a regular basis and see how their children grow and change as it happens, when my father returned home, he came back to the future.

In addition, what my mother knew depended on what we told her, and though I cannot speak for my brothers, I know that I did not tell my mother everything. I was selective in what I shared. I controlled my own narrative, often the only thing I thought I could control in my life.

Though I always thought it was hardest on the spouse and kids when Dad was away, my experience as a parent leads me to wonder what it must be like to come home to children who have changed and who are not the people they were when you last saw them.

Significant changes occur during the time a three-month-old baby grows into a toddler. And the differences between the fifteen-year-old me and the almost seventeen-year-old self my father met when he returned from Vietnam were as stark as day is to night. I know now from what my father has shared that for him, a daughter was a mystery, and I'm sure it was easier to let Mom take the lead. In many cases I found it easier too.

Dad and I did not discuss Mom except in the most detached way. I'd bring her up from time to time and so would he, but after a few sentences we'd stop. More than a decade had passed since her death and it was still too difficult for the two of us to talk about her. I knew he missed her, and I certainly did. But I also knew I still had feelings about the family dynamics that played out throughout my life and during the time between her diagnosis and the day she died that I had not worked out for myself, let alone with him. I wasn't convinced I needed to discuss that with him, though I suspected it would be a good thing. But I also knew that until he and I talked about Mom, what life was like when he was away from us, and my feelings about when she died, we would never really know one another.

CHAPTER 13

~

You and Your Mother

We'd been having tea, taking drives, and sharing memories for almost three years when Dad said, shaking his head, "You're just like your mother. You two had problems."

"Yes, at times we did," I responded, handing him a napkin with a cookie, and placing his tea on the table beside him. I sat down on the couch.

"It seemed like you always did," he said, muting the television and taking a sip from his mug.

"You know, Dad, all girls have problems and periods of time when they don't get along with their mothers. Rachel and her two girls have them, too. It's the way things are."

"If you say so," he said.

I bristled—not at being compared to my mother, but at what I saw as criticism of how I "handled Mom." While I didn't like what my father said, I blamed his being absent at critical times and his having only heard Mom's side of the story most of the time, so I gave him some slack as I always had about this topic. But when from time to time one of my brothers said it, I wanted to shriek,

"Are you kidding? You were there. You lived with us. I am *nothing* like her." Of course, I did not.

I remembered feeling as though the spats between my mother and me were an inconvenience to the men in our family. They acted as though our arguments were frivolous, stirred up the waters and rocked the family boat. Frankly, what went on between Mom and me was far more of an inconvenience to us.

Frustrated at Dad's lack of understanding, I remained silent. I'd told him all the things I loved about Mom and explained the reasons behind some of our arguments during afternoon tea and rides in the country. I just sipped my tea or looked out the window and changed the subject.

My mother would have said I was just like my father in that.

$$\sim$$

Growing up, I thought of her as restrictive, overly protective, and tougher on me than my brothers, especially during my teenage years. I was convinced that as my mother she *had to* love me, but that in reality she didn't like me at all.

My mother was a contradiction to me. Sometimes she would blow up for what I considered insignificant reasons having nothing to do with me. Yet, when I had to tell her about a serious matter, she would listen intently and then question me thoughtfully. After studying me calmly, she would formulate a strategic and reasonable way we would deal with the crisis "together."

She would coach me to keep things to myself while sharing too much with me about her personal feelings or emotions. At times she would share things and say, "Never tell your father." Sometimes she wouldn't talk to me. I knew at those times she was sad or angry about something that had nothing to do with me, but felt she was taking it out on us.

$$\sim$$

As a child I kept track of all of Mom's sins as a list of promises made to my future children. I would never make a scene at the post exchange where everyone knew us and knew who my father was. I would never purposefully embarrass my child in front of her friends just to demonstrate that I could. I would let my children decide how long their hair should be and how to wear it. I would let them choose their own clothes. I wouldn't refuse to drive my child somewhere at the last minute, so that eventually she had to quit an activity or give up going out, just to keep her at home. I would not search through my children's closets or dressers, read their diaries, or intercept their mail, read it, and not give it to them.

My issues with my mother were a big ball of wax, while my father and I dealt with one thing at a time. No big deal. But Mom's and my issues had been more complicated than my father could ever have known because she was a complicated woman, and I grew into one.

~

I would never think of sharing that litany of transgressions with my father, who I imagined would look at me and say, "For Chrissake. You're over sixty. Your poor mother's dead. Get over it. No one is perfect."

But I did want him to know the wonderful things I knew about my mother, like knowing that no matter how angry or upset something she did made me, it was almost always when she was alone with three children in a strange new place while he was away. And yet, somehow, I knew what she did had nothing to do with her not loving us. She loved us. Powerfully. Even when I thought it was far too much.

My brothers and I benefited from a woman who, no matter where we were in the world, read, researched, and explored every new place we lived and its surroundings until she knew every nook and cranny, its history, why it was important, and how it always, somehow, related to our life in some way. I have memories and the photograph of sitting close to my mother, who held my brother on her lap, on a hill in Germany after a picnic as she pointed to a hamlet below, hugged me tight against her, and said,

"Look, see that town? That's Bremen. Remember the Bremen Town Musicians? Name the animals in that band, Nancie."

I cherish the memory of her showing up one afternoon at my high school in Texas, my two brothers in the car, and whisking us away as a surprise.

"Where are we going?"

"Wait! You'll love it. I promise!" she said. And soon, we sat together under a makeshift tent in the Texas desert at a long wooden table with strangers and shared authentic Tex-Mex food. There we smeared freshly made, warm tortillas with the salsa and guacamole that sat in large bowls on the table we shared and talked with people we didn't know and would never see again. I could never do that on my own, even now. But she could. And she did.

If my mother determined that a teacher had treated one of her children unfairly, she'd charge into the school with the force of the 4th Armored Division, guns blazing. One summer evening as my family visited my father's parents out on Long Island along with some other relatives, my grandfather's cousin—an English professor at a New England university—responded to something I said with, "The last thing I need to hear is some young snit's opinion about some subject she knows nothing about."

My mouth dropped open. I looked down and continued eating. I said nothing for the rest of the meal. No one said anything at the time, but later in the kitchen as I was scraping plates in the sink, my mother came over to me and said, without lowering or raising her voice, without worry about who might overhear her, "Nancie. You are not a snit, but that woman is a cranky, unkind bitch. I'm surprised that as an English professor at a fine institution whose life's work is teaching young people, she is not more careful with her choice of words and knowing the real meaning of them."

I shared that story with my father.

"I remember that," he said. "I nearly said something, but your mother looked at me, so I didn't. She knew it would not end well."

I also told him about how, when she'd come home from Korea to bury her father, I took her with me (at her insistence) to a follow-up appointment when an ob-gyn told me I'd need to have an ovary removed and while they were in there they might as well take the other one as well. She said nothing until we walked outside.

"I'll never have children," I said.

"He's a drunk, Nancie," she responded. "You're fine." And she made an appointment for me to see a specialist at Hershey Medical Center, drove with me over two hours for my appointment, and said, "I knew it," when the specialist there said, "I don't know what your doctor saw, but there's nothing there now. It's a miracle."

~

Later that day I walked into his den and said, "Dad, I need to talk to you."

I sat on the couch and looked at him. He muted his ball game.

"When you say that Mom and I had problems, it bothers me. You and my brothers act as though Mom and I never got along at all. We did have problems, but you all act like I didn't love her or appreciate her. You may have witnessed some arguments and those are easy to remember, but you weren't there when I was growing up. You don't know the things that took place—the good things *and* the bad things.

"My mother and I had secrets even you don't know. Things she knew I'd never tell you and won't. We may have fought, but that's not unusual between mothers and daughters. Sometimes it's the only way a daughter can detach and come into her own.

"When I had my babies, it wasn't you I thought about or wanted with me. It was Mom. You don't know how much I miss her or how hard her death was for me."

By this time, I was crying and, I'm sure, wearing my ugly crying face. I couldn't look at him. He was quiet and when I looked up, he was sitting in his chair looking at me. Paying attention.

"I really loved Mom, Dad. And I knew she loved me."

Dad nodded. I got up to leave, just as he started to say, "Your mom's death . . ." Then he stopped. I stood by his chair looking down. He didn't go on. I was afraid he'd cry.

"Want some tea?" I asked. "I think I'll get some tea."

"If you're having some," he said. "That would be great."

CHAPTER 14

~

Don't Ask, Won't Tell

A FTER LIVING WITH DAD for a while, it finally occurred to me that what I knew about him had been learned from my grandmother, my mother, his brothers, my aunts, soldiers he'd commanded or served with and, of course, what I picked up during those times I'd lived with him growing up. I found his sharing of personal history entertaining and enlightening. I explained away what I didn't know. After all, we hadn't always lived together, we certainly had not for the past forty years. He was not someone who talked about himself much, until recently, and we couldn't know everything about everyone, could we? What did surprise me were the things I thought he knew about me and did not.

In the evenings after dinner, I would join him while he watched television. Some nights I worked on projects I had not been able to get to during the day because of phone calls or meetings.

"What are you doing over there?" my father asked from his recliner one night while watching his beloved New York Yankees play.

"Spreadsheets." I answered. "It's regional strategy time at work. We hold them each quarter."

"Where did *you* learn about spreadsheets?" he asked.

I ignored the surprised tone in his voice. Math had not ever been my strong subject. By the time I was in third grade, I became aware of my parents' unspoken expectation about my math capabilities after my father spent about an hour trying to explain fractions to me. That homework session with him ended in a question that I internalized as a statement about my intelligence. My exasperated father raised a frustrated voice we seldom heard and asked, "What are you? "What are you? A mental pygmy?"

I knew what a pygmy was, I'd read about them in *National Geographic*. I'd seen them in movies. They were small people. I understood at that moment that in my father's view, at least where math was concerned, maybe other things, too, I was a small, dumb person. Still, I benefited from that exchange because from that day on, if I did my "best" and earned As and Bs in all other subjects involving words (English, history, German and Mandarin, for instance) then a C in math-related subjects was acceptable. C minus, no; C, yes.

"Well," I answered. "When I was the comptroller for the Consortium of Universities . . ."

I saw his expression and held up my hand, "Don't say it, Dad," I warned.

"Why would they have hired *you* for that job?" He said it. I ignored its sting by laughing and saying, "I am really good at job interviews. But as I was saying, I computerized their accounting system when I worked there, plus I discovered Lotus spreadsheets. But I really learned to do analysis and other fancy things with them in graduate school when I worked on my MBA."

My father looked at me like a psychiatrist evaluating which ward in the asylum he should admit me to, because I was most certainly delusional, if not a pathological liar.

"You did not work on your MBA," he said, gently. He might as well have said, "Honey, listen to me, your name is Nancie, not Joan of Arc. You live in Maryland. Not France." He thought I was yanking his chain.

I wondered whether it was better he believed me insane or a liar. I opted for insane. I took a breath.

"Dad, I worked on my MBA in the evenings after work back in 2004-2005 . . . I think."

He stared at me.

"Really, Dad." His expression tickled me. A graduate degree in business was something even I would never have anticipated tackling, but the company I worked for at the time offered a tuition reimbursement benefit and I took advantage of it. In the technical and sales-related context of the place where I worked, my area of expertise was considered "soft." I'd grown up having to learn about different cultures and languages. Maybe if I had a better understanding of where I worked, and what the departments did in terms of business and product development, things would run more smoothly for me. I thought I might leverage an MBA for growth (and some respect). In addition, I eventually wanted to move back to the world I knew best and where I felt most comfortable—higher education or other nonprofits.

"Your mother would have told me." Never was it more concrete to me how much I'd relied on my mother to be collector and conduit of information from me to my father. Over the years—out of habit, laziness, or lack of courage—I'd left it to my mother to give my father information.

I wondered why she had not told him about this since she and I had discussed my plan to go to graduate school at great length. She'd expressed concerns about the extra layers of stress and work to my overwhelmed life as well as her worry about my health. Most of all she could not understand why I'd pursue an MBA rather than an MFA.

"Why do you always choose the most difficult path and make things harder for yourself than you need to?" she'd asked. "If you must go back to school, why not a concentration in writing? That would make more sense. You're good with words. An MBA is ridiculous."

I chalked her reaction up to motherly concern and a lack of knowledge and experience with the corporate world. Sometimes the easy way was not an option and sometimes you have to do what you have to do.

"Dad, she knew. Would you like to see my transcript?"

"No." He paused then said, "You didn't finish did you."

And there it was. My patience ebbed. I took this as an accusation and reminder of all the foolish decisions I'd made, the things I've tried and didn't complete, things where I failed miserably when I had been warned ahead of time not to try. I tried not to be hurt or angry. "No, I didn't finish," I said. I waited.

"Why not?" he asked.

"Because, Dad, I was two to four courses away from completing the degree when I had the strongest feeling that if I continued working and raising three children while carrying that heavy course load that I would die within six months. I was sure I'd drop dead from exhaustion or have a heart attack. I took a leave of absence and about six weeks later I had the mini-stroke."

There was silence. I broke it by stating, "I can't believe Mom didn't say anything."

"She didn't," he replied. Then he changed direction. "You never really told us things. We always found out things some other way."

I got the reference. As they wheeled me from the ER to my room after I suffered the mini-stroke, I'd given my two oldest daughters instructions. "Do not tell anyone yet. Do not call your father, my friends, the Marching Band Outreach Committee. Not anyone. And, under no circumstances should you call Grandma and Grandpa." At my instruction, the cone of silence descended.

It's easy now to wonder what I was thinking at the time, but I am sure I needed to understand fully what was happening myself. I worried that in trying to help, either my ex-husband or my parents would try to step in and take over. God forbid they should meet on the doorstep and struggle over who should take care of the children and me.

I recollected that I called my parents after my three-day stay in the hospital once I knew things were back to "normal." I'd learned that there was no residual damage, and I'd been informed that with changes in diet and lifestyle I'd be fine. My father claims that my mother called for a random chat and my eldest Rachel's boyfriend, Jon (now my son-in-law), answered the phone and told them I was in the hospital. My father said my mother asked Jon if they should come down. Dad says Jon said, "You should come."

It doesn't matter whose version was accurate. What matters is that Dad was correct. I often chose not to tell parents or others important things.

"I'm sorry, Dad."

"That's in the past," he shrugged. He continued to watch the game for a while before asking, "Why an MBA? Why make things hard for yourself? You'd have had more fun getting a degree in writing."

"That's what Mom said," I laughed. "Exactly that."

Though I was curious about what information my mother had not shared with Dad, I didn't wonder why. We knew now that Mom had been ill for far longer than we'd realized. And prior to that she and Dad had been caring for Dad's father until he moved to the nursing home. Moving forward it was my job to make sure I shared everything with Dad that he needed and wanted to know. And I was aware that it would take me a long time to share one of the things that was hardest for me to talk to my father and brothers about.

PART IV

I closed the box and put it in a closet. There is no real way to deal with everything we lose.

—Joan Didion, *Where I Was From*

CHAPTER 15

❧

Full Disclosure

ONE SATURDAY or Sunday after a short road trip to "just get out of the house," Dad and I sat at a table at one of the many diners on the Eastern Shore and enjoyed a cup of tea with dessert: ice cream sundae for him, Smith Island cake for me. We watched some kids run back and forth from the arcade games in the lobby to their parents' table for more quarters.

"Do you ever think of going out with someone again? Don't you miss having a companion?"

I was not only surprised that my father—the man who to me growing up had seemed determined I would be with no male person and who knew my history—asked this question, but also by the vehemence of my response, "NO! I do not."

Both of us were taken aback by my reaction.

"Well," he laughed, "you don't have to get mad about it."

"Dad," I said, softening my tone, "why would I want or need to get involved with anyone at this stage in my life? I've been married twice. I'm batting zero. Obviously, I'm not good at marriage."

"You're just not good at choosing husbands," he corrected me.

I frowned at him, paused, and then said, "I don't agree. I think they were both good men at heart. They and I just weren't as good at handling things as we might have wanted to be."

Years of thinking about it all had made me realize that they were each as good a prospect for marriage as I was back then.

"I'm not sorry I married either of them. I'm sorry that the marriages and the relationships afterward didn't work out. But anyway, I've been married. I've had my children. They're grown. I have grandchildren. I have my friends. I have my writing. My solitude. I have you. What else do I need?"

He looked at me, unconvinced. But nodded at me anyway.

Truth be told, I never thought about having another man in my life. Since the last marriage ended, as a reaction rather than a well-thought-out decision, I'd just accepted, if not decided, that I would never date again, let alone remarry. I began to think about why.

Most of my divorced or widowed friends were still filling out online dating profiles or getting matched up with someone by other friends. I just hadn't been interested. Was it because I hadn't seen anyone that interested me? Was I low on hormones? Why did people think women had to have a partner? My mother had referred to it as "Noah's Ark Syndrome."

Sometimes I worried that I was being selfish. I liked solitude. When people asked me if I missed having a man in my life, someone to care about or to care about me I answered, "I have been lucky to genuinely fall in love with two men and marry them. It was wonderful while it lasted. I'm satisfied that I had that experience. To have had the experience of loving them as much as I did . . . that was enough."

Maybe I had had to pack things up, leave the home I was in for a new one, unpack my stuff, and rearrange it to fit in with someone else's stuff far too often. Maybe I was just tired of everything. I was sure I had unresolved issues to deal with before any new entangling alliances. I planned to resolve them. That had to begin with understanding who I was, where I was, and how I got there without anyone else involved. I refused to think about the time and energy required or the complications that romance added to my already overwhelming life.

∿

A little more than twenty years earlier, life as I'd known, understood, and loved it changed in the space of a ten-minute conversation one day. The children were playing outside, and I sat on our family room sofa as I did each Sunday morning, reading under a large picture window through which sunlight poured in. Summer flowers—geraniums, petunias, and hibiscus—and herbs filled various sized pots on the deck outside. Classical music played in the background. I have a very tangible memory of looking up from what I was reading while sipping on a mug of tea and surveying the back deck and yard. I thought how lucky I was, even with all that had gone on for the past few years. A few minutes later, my husband, a man I'd loved more than any other, told me he thought he was gay.

∿

My husband and I had faced one challenge after another since 1987. Diagnosed with breast cancer, my mother underwent surgery for a mastectomy. My husband's parents died—his father within days after our youngest daughter Jane's birth and his mother a month after that. In addition, my husband's mentor with whom he had worked for more than fifteen years moved on to another position and not too long after died unexpectedly.

The fact that my husband's career suffered ups and downs for several years should not have surprised anyone after all he'd been through, but for a man, like many men, whose identity and sense of self seemed so tightly bound to his career, I understood this to be devastating for him, especially with the responsibility of a family. I thought I understood his depression. It seemed an appropriate and normal reaction to an abnormal situation.

I saw all of this as an opportunity—a chance to sell everything, move on, decide then what he really wanted to do, and create a new life for all of us. I'd have followed him anywhere. But that was my own approach to life. Not his. Instead he looked for like positions at the same salary and did everything to avoid selling the home he loved. One position after another for the next few years ended.

After majoring in miscellaneous for about twenty years, I had worked to finally complete my degree at Georgetown University. I finished my thesis with a concentration in literature and I was encouraged to immediately enroll to go on for my masters with the plan to teach a course on my topic, "The Institution of Motherhood: Representation of the Mother in Western Literature." Under other circumstances, this would have been a dream come true, but I had three small children, one barely a toddler, my husband had left his job, and I didn't feel it was time. I attempted to launch a writing career. I submitted essays, contributed chapters to three books, and edited another, which I could do from home. But soon, I returned to work as a manager for special projects for a small trade association that advocated for adults with disabilities. I only earned about one quarter of my husband's salary, but we needed medical benefits.

The abnormal became normal for us. We dealt with everyday issues together—taking care of the children, the yard, the house, what we presented to others—but there remained very little time or energy for one another. For what we considered the right reasons and, perhaps, because we both avoided topics that might result in conflict, we kept too much to ourselves during that time. It was one more thing we shared.

Despite my belief that we had a close relationship and shared everything, I always knew there was something he struggled with internally, based on what I observed as a certain wariness. It seeped through my husband's calm and confident façade, through which even I could not find an opening. This seemed at times to block total emotional intimacy with me, and with others. It belied my belief that I knew everything about him—at least my belief that I knew all I needed to know. I knew and accepted him as a reserved man where emotions were concerned. I ignored what others might have seen as red flags. I believed relationships grew through discovery. I respected his need for space. I knew I needed mine. Shouldn't every individual have some thoughts and feelings all their own?

I think now that I recognized in him what I knew about myself. There was much I held inside, too, preferring the internal, personal struggle if there was going to be one—so I did not analyze it. When he was ready, I trusted him to tell me.

In the last few years of our marriage there were growing signs of discordance and distancing, sudden and surprising sensitivity, and rage on the part of my typically strong, calm, quiet, and thoughtful husband to my or others' words or actions. I thought we just needed time, that having a job again, and working through his grief and all the changes would help. And things did seem to get better and start to level out when he returned to work.

Love was all we needed. We had that. Right?

Apparently not.

~

My husband went for a long bike ride every weekend morning. That morning, before leaving, he pulled the hassock near the couch as he always did, then sat down to put on his shoes before leaving. This was ritual.

While he shook foot powder into his shoes, we always talked a few minutes before he rode away. He'd let me know the route he was taking, when he'd be back, and we talked about what we might do later in the day. This morning he said, "I need to tell you something."

I put down the newspaper and looked at him.

He said, "I think I'm gay." He continued to fiddle with his shoes, looking at me now and then as he would have done had he told me that he thought we should think about sealing the deck again before summer, but I sensed his vulnerability and worry.

I looked at my husband as he sat across from me. While I might have expected to feel shocked or angry, I did not. Instead, I felt what a terminally ill patient must feel—that initial sense of relief when the doctor says, "I know what's wrong," just before revealing how much time one has left to live. I do remember thinking, "Our marriage is over."

I felt protective of him in that moment. I thought about what two people who loved and were committed to one another should say at a time like this. I thought about all we'd been through the past few years. I thought how hard—how frightening—it must have been to tell me this. I wondered how long he had struggled with when and how to tell me. I felt grateful that he trusted me enough to tell me. I wondered how I could not have known that my husband was gay. I wondered when he first knew.

I was very certain I did not want him to be afraid. I didn't think there was anything worse than feeling afraid. I was afraid then, but in a perverse way this realization led me to believe that we would somehow—based on this shared knowledge and experience—draw strength and forge a partnership, maybe different than the one we had, which would be solid and loving and safe.

I know I felt nothing but love for him at that moment. I was sure the two of us would make the best of this situation. I had faith in that and in him, so I said, "If that is true, we will handle this together. You'll be safe." Then I hugged him and thought I felt him relax. I sensed relief.

~

I do not remember much of what happened between his disclosure and when he left for his bike ride. But I do remember that after he left, I thought it odd that I wasn't shaking or crying or taking to my bed. This was serious. Aside from a Lifetime movie or two (and I had not liked the endings to those movies), I had no point of reference for how to deal with this situation.

Confronted with a serious problem, I did what I always do. I thought up possible scenarios—with narratives—for how we could work this out. I wanted to be sure we had options to discuss and choose among. Together.

Thinking up scenarios is my first line of defense in crisis. It's as though my mind separates from my emotions and body. Like a great narrator in the sky, an internal soundtrack starts, "Nancie walks to the kitchen, boils some water, pours herself a cup of tea, then moves to the sink and stares out the window as she plots her next steps. . . ."

Not that planning isn't important and necessary, but a person should be allowed to stop for a moment and say something like (take your pick):

"*Holy shit!*"

"How do *I* feel about this?"

"How did I miss that someone I've known for almost two decades is gay?"

"We had two children together."

"Oh my God! What will happen to us now?"

"The children. What about the children?"

"How and what do we tell the children?"

"*When* do we tell the children?"

"What should I do?"

"What do I want to do?"

And again, "*Holy shit!*"

But that's never really been my process. My process is more like, "Oh, there's a problem? Okay. Let's think about this. What are our options? Here's what we do. What do you mean, what am I feeling? Say nothing until we have a plan. There's time for feeling later. Maybe."

I know that initially, for a few seconds, I felt a sense of relief. I thought that now, at least, we both knew the situation we were dealing with and everything would be fine. We would handle it together. The problem was, we did not know what was to come. How could we? It took almost two years to run systematically, in the most civilized way, through our end-of-marriage to-do list. Toward the end, it became increasingly more difficult to remember a time when we both loved each other, let alone cared about one another. I cannot speak for him and would not presume to, but it became hard for me to believe he had ever really liked me and even harder to believe that if he ever had, he still did.

~

I looked at my father as he studied the check and pulled bills from his wallet. It occurred to me that maybe he wanted me to get involved with someone, date, get married again, and move out of his house. No. That wasn't it.

"Dad, what made you ask me that?"

He looked up at me for a moment, slapped a generous tip on the table and started to stand up before saying, "I just wondered if you get lonely. A little companionship is a nice thing. You don't have anyone around here."

"Do you ever wish you had someone to catch a movie with?" I asked.

"I think it would be nice," he said, "but I wouldn't ever want to get married again, and I think many women want to get married. I married your mother. She's my only wife. And, besides, I could never go through losing someone again. I just couldn't do that."

I nodded. He and I weren't so different. We didn't take risks when it came to emotions and love. We were all in or not at all. And once in, we were there for the duration.

CHAPTER 16

~

An Unsatisfactory Situation

AD'S QUESTION about whether I thought about or wanted a "companion" made me think. I checked in again with my unmarried girlfriends. They were of mixed minds. Some, like me, said, "Hell, no! Not at this stage of my life." But most missed having the company—not necessarily marriage, but someone they could share the joys of travel, theater, food, or nature with. I thought about what I missed about having a husband.

I missed hugs. I missed slow dancing. Dancing is like a moving hug with music. I liked leaning up against someone and having him wrap his arms around me. I missed feeling as though I fit perfectly within someone's embrace, close against him, as though there were no space between us at all, just part of them, skin to skin, the physical warmth, feeling his heartbeat. That feeling when it seemed my own heart began to beat in rhythm to his. I missed knowing someone other than my girlfriends, children, or father cared about and missed me when I wasn't there. When I thought about what I really missed it wasn't about being married.

I missed aspects of the relationship. The jokes, the shared history, the favorite songs, places, and moments only we knew.

Dad's question made me entertain the idea at least of a friendship with another man. Yet it also made me think about the end of my second marriage—something I had not and wasn't capable of doing to the extent I should have when it happened.

～

On reflection now, my heart still hurts for the two of us then. Had I paid attention to what I was feeling or been capable of feeling anything after my husband's disclosure that Sunday morning, I'd have recognized the early stages of grief and might have handled things differently. Now I am more able to see that I could not have possibly understood what he confronted.

As best I could, I presented my "we can do this and we can do it well" face, when I wasn't flat on my back on the couch listening to Bonnie Raitt sing "I Can't Make You Love Me" over and over. While I experienced shock and denial, my husband seemed to easily embrace and accept that he was gay. Even if he did not have specific plans to lead a new life at that time, one he'd had to deny for too long, I knew he could not and should not be prevented from living it.

I replayed our conversation over and over. I parsed what he said.

Talking to myself, I'd say, "He said, 'I *think* I *might be* gay.' He didn't say, 'I *am* gay.' Maybe he isn't really gay and just thinks he is for some reason." Then I'd try to think what those reasons could be. In those days, and for the first time in my life, I grasped for ambiguity over certainty.

I searched my memory of the time before our marriage. Had I missed hints that he was gay? There was nothing that I would have pointed to. Nothing I would have seen as a red flag. As someone who had lived all over the United States and lived in or visited other countries, my approach to measuring or categorizing others differed from a lot of people I knew.

My husband wasn't interested in watching football, basketball, or baseball teams, unlike my father, brothers, and many friends and neighbors' husbands. He was athletic—a runner and long-distance bicycler. He liked to garden and cook. Where my friend's husbands could not care less about the color of paint or wallpaper they put on the walls, I enjoyed his interest. Given his talent at and willingness to do all painting, I thought that only fair.

He was more fastidious than I. While he took great care in his appearance, I did not. My not caring about those things as a woman didn't make *me* gay, did it? It didn't occur to me to assign any label to him. As one of my friends said, "I love how he is so comfortable with his feminine side while you are cool with your masculine side. You balance each other out."

Okay. That made sense. And, by the way, the term 'metrosexual' appeared in our lexicon about that time. I thought he was trendy, in fact—avant-garde.

We were both creative. He excelled at the visual arts and design. My creative endeavors were focused on the written word and music, though he loved music, too. I saw creativity as more of a force within him than I think he did then. Because our talents and interests meshed as well as they did, nothing stood out. But really, why would or should it?

I felt that he was the first man in my life who seemed to appreciate my mind as much as my body and how I looked. Was that a gay thing? I didn't think so. I was just lucky. Right? That made me love him even more. I found it respectful.

I did remember a time during the first year after we were married when he came home one Sunday with a pierced ear. I jokingly asked him if there was something that he wanted to tell me. Obviously annoyed, he'd given me an indignant response, "No!" I took the earring in stride as another example of my husband's strong sense of individuality and not caring what anyone else thought. I admired that trait in him, too.

After revisiting the past to see where I'd missed clues, I started to bargain.

Maybe he wasn't "totally" gay but on the lower end of the spectrum. Maybe he was bisexual. But all that did was provide a possible explanation for why he'd married me. Then I decided it might be easier for all of us if he were just gay. It was clearer cut. In the end, my mind always returned to how after almost twenty years of knowing this man and almost fifteen years of marriage, I could not have known my husband was gay. Or why he finally chose to tell me after all that time. Eventually I became mentally and emotionally spent.

I did not want to be angry at him, just the situation. After exhaustive sessions of overthinking, during which I tried to come up with answers to all my questions as well as any that others might ask me, I would turn in another direction. What if he were not my husband? What if he were a relative, friend, or neighbor who chose to tell me this?

That made things easier. I did not believe that someone chose to be gay. I understood how familial, religious, and societal pressures would prevent someone from disclosing this. In that frame of mind, for brief moments of strength and understanding, I held anxiety and anger at bay. In those moments of clarity, I understood that it was unfair to expect someone to be who they were not or to live a life that wasn't the one they were meant to live. Still, fear about what the future held for me, the children and, indeed, him, lurked.

~

For a short time, we enjoyed a honeymoon phase. We attempted to start where we were then. Though I admit I wasn't happy about the situation, I was happy for him. He seemed more comfortable, less depressed, and even excited. Many times, I smiled to myself as I watched him approach this phase of life as he did all new projects. He read, studied, and talked to me about his thoughts on what he learned. To this he added joining support groups. I could not explain then, nor can I now, how easily my excitement for him and my own dread coexisted.

Though I was happy to see my husband's happiness for himself and the potential for his life ahead, it also pained me. I knew it meant that eventually I would move from co-traveler on the journey to bystander, whether he realized that or not. That time came far sooner than I thought.

~

"There's a group for gay married men," he told me. "I'm going to attend their next meeting. They go out to dinner at a nearby restaurant afterward."

"That's interesting," I said. "Sounds like a great resource." All the while my mood slowly edged forward from denial and closer to anger as I thought how lovely it was that the wives stayed home alone, taking care of the children, cooking dinner and cleaning up, while the husbands shared a dinner and drinks downtown. Then I'd snap out of it and think, "I'm such a bitch." I hoped when he met those men, he'd see that he was not gay after all.

The weekend after he attended the meeting, I answered the phone to hear a woman introduce herself.

"Nancie, your husband gave my husband your phone number. He attended the Gay and Married Men's Association meeting last week. He thought we might be a resource for you."

I said nothing before she recognized the silence and said, "You didn't know that I'd be calling. I'm sorry."

As she told me about the group of women who were married, separated, or divorced from gay men, I came to understand that she knew exactly where I was in this process and how I felt. She encouraged me to join them at their next meeting.

"To be honest, this is all so new to me," I said, "that I don't know what to think or what to do yet."

"You don't have to promise anything. Come when you're ready. And please do not hesitate to call before that if you need to talk."

She gave me the date of the next meeting, then added, "By the way, for your first meeting it's not necessary, but we do ask each woman to bring a dessert. After we meet, we socialize."

I sensed a shift in my feelings. Where I'd been edging from denial to anger from my husband's disclosure up until just a few minutes before, I was now up to my ears in rage. No more denial. I was married to a man who was gay.

My husband looked at me expectantly as I hung up the phone and turned to him.

"You gave them my name?" I practically snarled. "And my number?"

"Oh, I forgot to tell you about the Straight Spouse's group. One of the guys suggested it. He said he'd have his wife call you."

I began to laugh and noticed his expression had changed from hopeful to wary.

"You realize that outed me, right?" I asked. My raised eyebrows and half smile belied a seething swirl of emotions, menacingly close to the surface.

I realized fully for the first time that though I'd known I was along for the ride while someone else drove, I would have no say in determining the speed at which we traveled.

"I'm really sorry," he said, genuinely apologetic. "I thought it would be helpful. I thought a group of women going through what you're going through would be a good support for you."

I was not laughing by this time. I turned my back on him and walked away.

"Oh and by the way," I snapped, "I think it's typical and ridiculous that you men have a night on the town, get drinks and dinner at a nice restaurant after your meeting, yet expect your wives to stay home, take care of the children, make their dinner, and clean up when we have to bring our own damn dessert to our meeting."

I walked away. Then, over my shoulder, I said, "I will *not* arrange for babysitting."

"So you'll go?" he asked.

"Maybe," I responded.

~

He told his family and close friends first. A few called me after he spoke to them. Though I was so appreciative that they thought to call me after hearing from him, a ringing phone threw me. I had a hard time knowing what to say. Sometimes after a few minutes of banter, I'd begin to cry, then quickly recover, and try to put on a brave front. One friend said, "Oh, Nancie. You still love him."

Of course I did. It would have been easier for both of us had I not.

I called my mother, and after the typical, "How are you and Dad?" I told her the news. I cannot remember what I said, but I'm sure I was very calm—as though it were just another typical day at our house and the water heater had gone out. "Mom, I have something I have to tell you."

I do remember that there was a short silence. And then, "How are the two of you? This had to be extremely hard. For him to tell you and for you to hear it."

I told her everything I knew—that we still cared about one another, that we were committed to working on it together, we were still friends, family. We wanted the children to be affected as little as possible. No, they didn't know.

Looking back now, it's hard to fathom how naïve I was. But I was relying on defense mechanisms I'd utilized my whole life. Break things down into pieces the size you can handle. Order them. Put away the ones you don't have to deal with now. At some level I knew that once again I'd be leaving the life I knew and marching into a new one. But right then, I just needed to deal with the information we had at the time and process that.

My mother called back on Monday morning to check in and to let me know she'd told my father.

"What did he say?" I asked.

"He said he was sorry. But that gay or straight, he's still the same man we've known."

From then on, Mom was the conduit between me and Dad for information about what was happening. Not that I couldn't have talked to him about it; it just seemed that Mom and I did all the communicating. That was not unusual. It had always been the case.

~

We agreed to tell the children together, but I felt we needed to wait longer than he did. They were fourteen, ten, and seven.

I did not believe the girls were ready or that they could understand our decision to separate. I did not know how much we should tell them. I worried that they were too young to understand the reasons why. I think now that I still hoped he'd come to me one day and say, "I'm not gay after all. I *thought* I was because . . . ."

But I underestimated and did not anticipate the urgency behind my husband's need to tell the children so soon. Had I tried to hold off until we worked out our relationship and processed how his being gay changed that first? Honestly, I still hoped this was a phase.

In hindsight, I see that prior to his disclosure, our relationship had changed and been deteriorating slowly. His being gay was not the only issue. Even if he had not stopped caring about me entirely, his feelings for me had shifted. I felt like a distant relative. And I remember questioning whether he even liked me at all, let alone loved or cared about me. Again, rather than ask, I brushed off my concern and filled the gaps in our relationship with child-related activities, classes, volunteer work, and my new job.

Soon, I felt like a reflection in his rearview mirror. While I remained, rooted stubbornly to the landscape of what had been our life together, he wanted to move on to meet me in a new place. I did not want to move, yet I could not stay either.

One day after returning from an event at our younger daughters' elementary school, I found my husband raking leaves in the front yard. It was then he revealed to me that he'd told Rachel he was gay. I stood for a moment, staring at him in disbelief.

"We agreed we would tell the girls together," I said while he looked at me as though confused as to why I would be upset. "Why didn't you wait for me to come home?"

That was the moment I accepted the impending end of our married relationship and the possible end to any relationship at all. I had not expected damage to what had been up to that time a solid parenting partnership. And I had not expected my own reaction to this first fissure in the foundation of it.

Internally, my reaction was more about a piece of territory I had occupied and guarded alone—one not really shared with anyone—the fear and anxiety that our current situation might provide my first husband and his wife a reason to sue for custody. There had never been any indication prior to this one that they felt inclined to that. There was no indication that there ever would be, but I had not discussed this with them yet and now I worried that my daughter would. In anticipation of our eventual separation and dissolution of the marriage it became and remained a point of high anxiety for me, one of my biggest fears.

~

Rachel had been two and a half years old when I married for the second time. Though she had done her best to keep him at arm's length during the first six months or so, her stepfather remained unflappable and consistent, eventually winning her over. He loved her as fully as Sharon and Jane, the two daughter,s we had together, always there for her after her every-other-weekend, alternating major holiday, and summer visits with her natural father. I venture to say that she and her sisters, like I, forget and must be reminded of their half-sibling status, so seamless was his love and care for them.

Without realizing it at the time, I shape-shifted then from spouse, friend, and partner to single mother. I stared at him briefly before turning to run across the lawn, up the porch steps, through the front door, and up the stairs to her bedroom on the second floor. My worry for my daughter overrode my fury at him.

I knocked at her bedroom door, not knowing what to expect. I looked into her eyes when she opened the door part way trying to determine her reaction. Her face was expressionless. No, not expressionless. It wore that expression one has when the person they're looking at has not met expectations. No disappointment, really, but more "Ah, well. What else did I expect?"

We talked for a few moments through the crack in the door until she said she wanted to be alone.

I made my way downstairs to the kitchen. I put the kettle on the stove. I needed tea. I didn't know what to do next or what I'd say to him. I just drank my tea and paced back and forth, wiping down the kitchen counter. Clearing things off the table. Picking children's things up off the floor. After he finished up outside, my husband came into the house and sat in one of the chairs in the family room. He made a few statements about how he thought the discussion with Rachel had gone. He felt her reaction less mature than he'd hoped. It was probably not the most mature thing for me to say, but I responded that she was fourteen and that her job was to be immature.

From then on I watched them both wondering how, and if, the two of them could ever rehabilitate their relationship. I wanted them to but realized that I had no dominion over that. I was not even certain he and I could manage that for ourselves.

That one incident changed how I approached each day from then on. I accepted that the marriage was over while hoping that we'd find some way to save at least parts of our relationship. I began to think about the steps we needed to take. I felt that my husband had begun to handle things on the advice of others or as he felt he needed to despite our long conversations and agreements about how to proceed. We were no longer in alignment about issues we'd once agreed upon. My focus changed from how he and I had been to how we should proceed to making what I thought were the best decisions for our children.

My ability to trust in him or anyone became harder and harder. My ability to be civil began to wane as well.

We finally told the younger girls that we were separating and as I expected they did not understand.

"But you never fight," our middle one, Sharon, said.

"You love each other," said Jane, the youngest.

"We still do," I assured them. "Things are different now. I understand that it is hard to understand. I'm so sorry."

I knew how they felt. It was all too hard to understand. Even for their mother.

~

Though we had not settled on a specific date—a year and a half had passed since his disclosure—it was clear that sometime within the next six months or so we would officially separate and sell our home. We began to tell our neighbors. For ten years, we had developed a close group of friends on the cul-de-sac where we lived. We couldn't have asked for better friends, and both of us felt supported and cared for by them. Past the confines of that small group, things were different.

There is a welcoming and supportive LGBTQ community that extends open arms to someone who comes out, but the straight spouse remains in the personal world the gay spouse leaves behind—and it is filled with prejudice and misunderstanding.

The private person that I am I began to feel exposed. Rumors were plentiful, people had questions. Some children were no longer allowed to play with mine. Some who were still allowed to play with them were not allowed to come to our home for birthday or slumber parties. Though my husband assured me that there had been no past or current relationship with anyone outside our marriage and I believed him, some people assumed that was not the case. I was told by one woman that I was lucky: "At least there isn't another woman." Others asked me if I'd been tested for HIV/AIDs. "You really need to go in right away. You never know!" It all became too much, and I retreated inward.

I was angry, no matter how hard I tried not to be. Despite my experience and skill at relocating and setting up new households, I resented the prospect of having to pack up the remnants of our life, the life I loved, to move to a new place, and begin to build a new life alone. I hated having to sell what had been our dream home, and having to find a new one that I could afford on my own in the same school district for our children, trying to answer the children's questions, supporting them, all the while maintaining a happy and "everything will be okay" front with my husband and everyone else. Once again, someone else's orders directed my being displaced.

My husband showed his disappointment, frustration, and anger at what he may have felt was my inability to be happier for him or trust that caring for us and being gay was not mutually exclusive. I don't know whether he had those thoughts. We didn't talk about them. As usual, I assigned reasons for his behavior toward me. As he offered ideas about how we could move forward, I listened while thinking of all the ways they could not work.

Slowly, I began to resist hearing about the groups he attended or the new people he was meeting. It seemed to me to portend of what was to come—him living a new life and having experiences I would not be part of.

He spoke about new people he met, some couples, like us, in which the husband was gay and the wife not. He shared the various ways they handled "life after the disclosure."

"They still live together in one house with their children."

I looked at him and asked myself, "How does that work? Do they meet once a week to talk about separate date nights and to schedule babysitting? Do they both date? What happens if one of them has a breakup. Is the other one expected to pick up the pieces?"

"This couple lives in the same house but he has the upstairs apartment with his partner, and she lives downstairs with the children and hers."

I began to develop a checklist for "next steps and moving on." When you've exercised all your options, make a to-do list, I always say. One Sunday afternoon, as we drank wine on the deck, I asked, "Where do you see this going? What do you think we should do? We obviously can't continue like this."

"I guess we should separate," he said, "and then file for divorce." He looked uncomfortable, and I realized that I had made that decision already but set up the situation so that he would have to be the one to initiate it.

I calmly pulled out my list. How calculated and passive aggressive it must have seemed to him that I would flaunt the evidence that I'd already decided on the direction we would take to end things. There, laid out in black and white, was everything I'd been thinking but not speaking about.

Leaving was something I knew how to do. So was leaving first. Never underestimate a military brat's ability to walk away and never look back, someone once said. Cut your losses, bite the bullet, walk away as you toss a live grenade over your shoulder. No gentle descent into the end of our story. Pretend it's easy, leave the field under your own power. There would be other battles on other days. What I didn't know was that I'd be my own worst enemy.

As we worked through the lists, I fought my negative feelings and tried to focus on the good things about him, about us. But I could not always stop the negative thoughts. I tried not to believe that he'd chosen to abandon us happily or that he'd chosen the time, waiting until pivotal people in his life were no longer with us so he could enter a whole new world where it was easy to deny he'd ever been in ours. But hardest to accept was my sense that he now saw me part of his enemy camp.

Sometimes I would say something and he'd nod knowingly, saying, "They said you would probably say that."

It enraged me. I wondered who the hell "they" were. Whoever they were, they had replaced me in his sphere of trust. They did not know him as well as I did, I thought. No one did, in my mind, completely discounting that I had never really known him either.

One night while discussing something, the topic of which I do not remember, he said, "I really don't care what you think."

I recoiled inside. Since his disclosure, my husband had always treated me with respect. I remember studying him for a few seconds to determine whether perhaps he'd had a mental breakdown from all the stress and did not recognize who he was talking to in that moment. This was not the man I knew. Not the man I'd married. Not my best friend.

I said slowly, "Do you know who I am?" as though my next question would be, "How many fingers am I holding up?" or "Who is the president of the United States?"

I asked in all seriousness, checking his expressions, body language, and affect for signs of mental distress.

He looked at me squarely and said, "Yes. I do. I know exactly who you are."

I felt threatened—not physically, but in the sense that I no longer held any place at all in a relationship with this man. He could not possibly be interested in working anything out. He was done, but I persisted. Still not convinced he wasn't suffering some sort of memory lapse, I asked again, "You know I'm Nancie. Your wife. The mother of your children?"

He stood up from the chair he was sitting in and walked toward me.

"Yes."

I looked up at him. "And you truly do not care how I feel or what I think?"

"No, I don't," he responded.

I saw the act of standing up and walking toward me as the first real phase of claiming ground of his own, pushing me away and out of his life. Just for a moment I wondered what I'd said that set him off. Maybe I had contributed to some sort of face-saving response in him by some expression or tone of voice.

And yet, suddenly, all fear and confusion left me. I stepped away and looked at him.

"Okay, that's all I needed to know," I responded, pleasantly, I think. Then I turned and walked away. He said nothing as I left the room.

It had been a while since I'd experienced such clarity. Years, in fact. I felt lighter. I accepted it as a gift. I slept downstairs and all the way through the night for the first time in a long time.

By the time I woke up the next morning, his bike was gone,

indicating he was on a ride. I was grateful for a couple of hours of alone time. I found a note from him on the kitchen counter when I went to grab a mug of coffee. It was a lovely apology for what he'd said and how he'd behaved the night before. He wrote that he didn't know why he'd acted in the way he had because I didn't deserve that from him. He wrote, "I love you."

I stared at the note. And then, I was pissed, but not because I didn't believe him or want to. It was because I knew it was over, that I would never get past his saying he didn't care what I thought or how I felt. Nothing he could say now would ever change that.

I tore the note up in little pieces, placed it in a small china dish, and lit it with a match. I watched it burn while I drank my coffee. Then I left the ashes in the dish on the counter where I found the note and went into the dining room to read the newspaper.

After his ride, he came into the dining room and sat down.

"Hi! Did you see my note?" he asked hopefully.

"Yes, I did." I said.

"Do you want to talk about it?"

I put down my paper and picked up my coffee mug.

"No, I don't," I responded.

Then I told him I thought he should find a place to live by January 2. That I did not want the children's Christmas disrupted and that we could talk about details of the move, the sale of the house, and all the other arrangements later. But for now, I had nothing else to say.

Later that day, I took the girls and we went shopping to buy new linens, a comforter set and accoutrements for the downstairs guestroom and bathroom.

They helped me make up the sleep sofa and arrange all my towels and toiletries in the bathroom. I tried to make it cheerful. I felt unburdened and wanted them to know I was okay.

Later my husband came downstairs. When he realized what I planned to do he said, "This isn't necessary. It's not right. You stay in the bedroom. I should move down here." But I wanted, I needed, to be the one who moved. I had everything I needed downstairs, especially the floor separating where the two of us would sleep until he left.

I began to take the girls to open houses so we could choose a new home together. It would be so hard for them to move. As a child I had promised myself that I would not make my children move a lot, or change schools, especially in the middle of the school year. I began to figure out when the house should go on the market so that they could end the school year in this house. And I looked for houses in the same school district so that they would not have to leave their friends and so we'd be moved in and settled before school started the next year. I wanted them to feel as though they had some say in *something*, even if it were just a new house. I wanted them to know I had not forgotten that this affected them, too.

～

Still, I tried to understand why I couldn't be more understanding about what he was going through. It finally dawned on me that I did not need to be married to him. I just didn't want to lose my best friend.

From the time of his disclosure, I had known that we could not remain married or continue to live together as he began to live life as a gay man. That's a different thing than accepting it happily. But I had hoped that the only thing that would change was his address and that I'd sleep alone. I wanted him to remain my closest friend. I wanted him to still want to spend time with me. Not just the children. I wanted him to come over and have dinner, call up and ask me to do things that friends do, all the activities we had enjoyed doing together both with the kids and without.

I did not want to think of him being smitten or in love with someone else. I knew what that was like. The thought of someone else in my place didn't make me jealous. It made me terribly sad. I had hoped we could evolve into "best friends with children." I was desolate when that didn't happen, and it appeared as though we would become a statistic, the stereotypical ex-spouses who did not get along.

We had discussed and worked out a plan for almost everything that needed to be handled prior to his leaving except one. We never discussed or settled on what we would be to each other when it was done.

In fairness to my husband, there were times in the beginning when he attempted to reach out or to comfort me. There were times during the years after that he tried. I rebuffed his gestures. Not because I didn't want the comfort or his care, but because when he left again, I'd miss it more.

I did not want to have to need him or rely on him, though I had grown to. I fell back on the only thing I knew to do in difficult times—pack away the pain, hide it in a closet of my own making and carry on. It hurt terribly that I missed him and needed him more than he did me.

For all our management skills and experience, despite all our years together, first as friends, then as spouses, we had not known how to navigate this new terrain and salvage any of what had brought us together in the first place. And though we were clear on who we were and who did what in terms of the children— schedules, responsibilities, etc.—we had not defined what we were to be to one another. We hadn't even discussed it.

~

Many years later, I went to his apartment to pick up one of the girls who planned to meet me after she finished work. He offered me a glass of wine, and we talked amiably while I waited for her to arrive. One of his neighbors casually walked into his apartment. Clearly, she was used to dropping by. He interacted with her easily, far more comfortably than he had with me in years. She wanted to fill him in on the status of another neighbor who had been hospitalized. Did I just imagine that he positioned himself in a way to block her view of me? As she glanced awkwardly at me and politely tried to include me in the conversation, I wondered how long he would pretend I was not in the room or that she didn't see me sitting on his couch with my glass of wine.

Finally, the woman walked toward me extending her hand, "I'm so sorry for interrupting your evening." My ex-husband looked as though he would jump in front of her to block one part of his world from touching the other. He said, "Oh, I'm sorry. This is Nancie. A friend."

"I'm Sharon and Jane's mother," I said, smiling as I reached out to shake her hand.

"Oh, I know your daughters. Lovely girls."

Lovely girls, as though I had to be told that. It felt very strange. I was hurt. A woman without a role. I was no longer his wife, not even his ex-wife, or even the mother of his children. I was "a friend"—not a best friend, not a good friend. What kind of friend was I?

After the woman left, I queried, "A friend? I'm your friend?"

I wasn't sure why the word friend seemed so insulting. Hadn't I hoped we would remain or at least grow into friends again? We had not and I did not realize it until that moment.

"I didn't know what to say," he responded, obviously as startled by his reaction as I had been.

"How about 'This is Nancie, my ex-wife' or 'This is my Nancie, my daughters' mother?'" I suggested. I tried to make light of it. I felt his discomfort. There was no point in coming up with a plan for a next time. There would be no next time as far as I was concerned. I'd make sure to stay outside of his universe, though he couldn't help but continue to be part of mine because of the children.

∼

I would describe our relationship after that as only children-centered. He backed me up if I called him in where discipline was necessary. He joined us for holiday and birthday dinners, for special events at school, traveled with us on team trips, and was indispensable if something needed fixing around the house.

Once in a while, in between apartments, he lived with us in our downstairs family area where guests stayed. Even then, we were not able to find our way to what I would define as friendship or even discuss the possibility of one.

For the next ten years, I redirected myself, my emotions in particular, to my work and my girls. My goal was to shepherd all three of them through high school and college as alive, happy, and healthy as possible, without drug problems or early pregnancies. Life went on and like a good soldier, I just kept marching through it.

After nearly ten years, I was not equipped emotionally to find a new way to relate to him and his new life. Nor was I able to even think about redefining a life for myself. I was still in too much pain. I began to think like a short-timer—a soldier coming to the end of one station and looking forward to another. My youngest would be graduating in June and off to college. I'd be an empty nester. I could live and work differently. I resorted to habit and thought about packing up and moving on. Leaving that place and arriving at a new one.

Then my mother died.

CHAPTER 17

～

Need to Know

SEVEN YEARS after the demise of my second marriage, I called my mother to catch up. Mom and I always spoke on the weekends at least. When she didn't answer I kept trying. After several attempts I began to worry, but Dad finally picked up the phone.

"Hi, Dad. How are you?"

"We've had some bad news," he said.

I expected him to tell me that my 102-year-old grandfather had died.

"Oh, no! What happened?" I asked.

"Your mother has cancer."

～

The first time a doctor at a nearby military hospital discovered a lump in my mother's breast she was forty-one. I was twenty-one. As with military medicine, she had to be referred for the biopsy and then wait for the appointment—a few days, a week or more, I don't remember—but I do remember the pall over our home and the fact that she and I did not discuss it. This matter was my parents' to deal with, so I didn't dare to ask, though I wondered how she felt—was she afraid? I wanted to tell her how I felt. I was afraid. Instead, I busied myself around the house to help.

I watched out the kitchen window as she lay in the cold, late fall weather in a lawn chair, buttoned up in her coat and scarf, wrapped in a blanket and alone in her thoughts. For at least two days she would go outside and stay there for hours. I see now that it was the one place she could be totally alone with thoughts and feelings. Thankfully, that time, we got the news that her lump was benign.

"Is she okay out there?" I asked my father.

"Let her alone," he'd say. "She needs that."

They found the next lump while my parents were in Korea. They were incommunicado for almost three weeks. After trying to reach them every day by phone from stateside, I finally did. My Dad told me that they had found another lump. Mom had gone to Hawaii for the biopsy, and it, too, was benign. I would not find out until later that the biopsy had been a traumatic experience for Mom. She thought she was having a needle biopsy (a new procedure then) rather than the invasive and deforming surgical biopsy the military doctors performed without her consent. When she finally saw the incision after the procedure, she felt that they had misled her and was both angry and depressed. I do not believe she ever got over that experience, despite being relieved that it was not cancer.

In 1987, while lying in bed and performing a self-exam, which my mother did religiously, she found another lump.

"She said, 'Lowen, I have a lump,'" Dad told me later, "I tried to feel it, but I couldn't. 'It's right here,' and she pointed to it, but I couldn't feel it. When the doctor looked at the results of her mammogram, he could barely see it. He said he wasn't sure how she found it."

This time it was cancer, so required a mastectomy. My husband and I encouraged Mom to have the procedure at Georgetown University Hospital's Lombardi Cancer Center. My husband worked at the University at the time and helped get her an appointment right away with one of the best surgeons.

The doctors let her know that they got everything, that no evidence of it spreading existed. Despite that, they recommended a short course of chemotherapy and radiation. Mom refused both.

Mom and I talked a lot this time, but she was far more focused on the fact that my third baby would be arriving in a few months. In my relief that she was okay and that her prognosis was good, it didn't occur to me to request that when things like this happened that she and Dad let me know right away and that dispensing important information on a "need-to-know" basis was upsetting and unfair.

~

Here we were again, nineteen years later, and the cancer came back. I knew that she'd had a physical scheduled that week. She'd been having back pain for some time. She believed that it was due to a fall from a tree during her childhood. Her primary care physician had ordered X-rays and referred her to an orthopedic surgeon.

"I was with her," Dad told me. "She always wanted me there when she talked to doctors, you know. She filled the doctor in on what had been going on, and he suggested she go over to the hospital for X-rays. She told him that she'd had those done the day before, so he went out of the room to call them up. When he returned with a nurse, I knew it was bad."

The surgeon let her know that cancer had metastasized. It was in her bones. He wasn't sure whether it was due to the breast cancer or the tumor in her pancreas.

"Wait," I interrupted him, "Breast cancer? And a pancreatic tumor?"

"We went back to her oncologist in Delaware, and he said, 'We can beat this, Suzanne.'"

"Dad, it's in her bones. What about the tumor in her pancreas? I don't understand. . . ."

He stopped me. "Nancie, the doctor said we can beat this. He's the doctor."

I knew my mother was going to die. Even if she only had breast cancer that had spread to her bones, it was a matter of time, but pancreatic cancer, in those days, gave patients a life expectancy of six weeks to six months.

Dad was insistent. The plan was to beat this. We would all follow the plan. I didn't attempt to breach the fortress he built around Mom and himself at that time. I followed his orders, avoiding a confrontation. I fell into step on the path through denial that my father cleared, paved, and directed my brothers and me to follow.

During the months that followed, I would call my younger brother—the middle child—to compare notes and, when I felt Dad wasn't listening to me, ask him to intercede with Dad. But Dad wasn't talking to him either. I was sure, since my younger brother lived at home at the time but had a long commute to Fort Meade each day, that Dad or Mom did not share much with him either.

CHAPTER 18

~

Hail and Farewell

I WANTED TO GO OUT to visit right away, but Dad said he'd rather I wait until they set up a routine and saw what Mom could deal with. He didn't want to disrupt her schedule. There was no surgery necessary since the breast cancer was located on the side where she'd had the mastectomy. According to Dad, they were going to focus on the breast cancer and deal with the pancreatic tumor later. She had doctors' appointments, radiation, and chemo treatments, which exhausted her.

I offered to take off work, but Dad and Mom said there would be time for that later. I didn't get a chance to talk to Mom on the phone at all during the weeks after the diagnosis; she was so tired from the ordeal she was under. Dad became primary caretaker, giving up everything to be with her and manage her days. Finally, Dad said I could come out to see them.

~

I arrived on a Friday night, as I usually did, then got up early the next morning to have coffee with Mom. We sat in their television room—Mom on the couch, me in a chair across from her. She was in her nightgown, me in mine. Looking at us, you'd have thought it was any other Saturday morning. I knew we occupied a small piece in time in a critical and fragile space. We had convinced Dad that he did not have to hover and that he should take advantage of my weekend visit to run errands, or, perhaps, take a nap. He'd seemed afraid to leave us.

Although she was in her nightgown and bathrobe, Mom wore her usual lipstick and earrings. I freshened our mugs of coffee: hers black with an ice cube, mine with milk. She sat on the edge of the sofa. I studied her. Her color was still good, though she looked tired and had lost some weight. I noticed the toes of her right foot curled slightly around the top of the left. A sign she was uneasy. Over time, I'd become used to looking at my mother's feet for signs of how she felt, as though her emotions fell to her feet where they might be solidly planted, unsteady, or moving nervously despite how composed the rest of her body appeared to be.

This was the first time she and I had talked since her diagnosis.

She learned forward on the sofa, and said, "I don't think I'll make it through this, Nancie."

I didn't hear what she said as a statement. I heard a question. I know now that she was telling me. She was not going to make it. I did not offer a reassuring, "Don't be silly. Of course, you will! They've made such strides in fighting cancer. You beat this before."

I knew she was going to die, despite the doctor's "We can handle this." What, exactly, could they handle? It didn't matter how positive my father tried to be. It didn't matter how strategic his battle plan, how precise the logistics he laid out, how hard he fought.

I was not going to lie to her. Not now. But if she didn't know or was not ready to know, I was not going to be the one to tell her. Instead, I leaned toward her and asked softly, "Mom, are you afraid?"

I remember noticing that my voice didn't sound as adult-like as I would have wanted. It sounded like a curious question that begged an honest answer. The kinds of questions I asked when I was a child and wanted her reassurance about something.

She stared at me as though surprised by my response. Maybe I imagined that. Maybe she was just being thoughtful. She leaned back on the sofa and stared out through the door that led to the patio outside the dark room into the sunny fall day. My eyes followed hers. It was clear and crisp outside. Branches filled with autumn colored leaves moved gently. Fall. How appropriate a time. . . .

"Of dying? No." Then with certainty she said, "No, I'm not afraid of dying. I loved and married your father. We had wonderful children."

I wanted to cry. I wanted to move to her side and hold her. Really, I wanted to have her hold me so we could both cry and rock together for comfort. But I didn't know how to do that or ask for that. We were not a family practiced in public displays of affection or any real outward expressions of emotion except through the filter of humor. Random eruptions of anger were viewed as a total lack of control. A cardinal sin.

"We lived all over the world," she said. Then she smiled at me. "Just two kids from Brooklyn." Her eyes wandered around the room—German steins on the mantel, cuckoo clocks on the walls, cloisonné and porcelain knick-knacks from Taiwan and Japan on the bookshelves, temple rubbings from Thailand, footrests made from camel saddles from someplace with camels, which held feet when not filled with magazines, my father's military memorabilia. She turned to me again. She seemed to relax. "I've had a good life. I'm satisfied."

We quietly sipped our coffee. How unusual for me not to try to fill the uncomfortable silence. I waited.

"I am afraid of the pain though."

I felt myself slip into a role more comfortable than the grieving daughter I was becoming. I morphed into attentive listener, observer of body language and facial expressions, sleuth of subtext, mirror to what she said. I was brave. I've always known that crippling fear can coexist with courage. It's just easier to display courage, even small amounts, in the face of fear and overwhelming sadness.

We talked about her fear of pain and the palliative measures available now, while my mind organized all the people and resources I could consult while displacing any of my own emotional pain. Suddenly, she blurted out, "My family is gone. My close friends who aren't dead live too far away. Who will give my eulogy?"

This time I was surprised. My mother was not afraid of death, but of being forgotten. This I could relate to, though I wondered how she thought anyone would not remember her.

"I will," I said, almost immediately. I almost regretted volunteering so quickly, not because I didn't want to write and deliver her eulogy, but I wondered if this was a rhetorical question. I wondered if that was what she really wanted. I wondered if I would have been the person she would have chosen if I had not volunteered. I wondered if I had put her in a difficult position in case there was someone that she would prefer to have eulogize her. And I wondered if I could even manage to deliver her eulogy if I wrote it.

"You will?" she asked. She seemed both surprised and happy.

I nodded.

"Really? Are you sure?"

"Yes, of course." And I was certain. I could write her eulogy. In that moment, I knew I was meant to do this. I began to think about it immediately: what I'd say, poetic references, funny stories.

Six months later, during my mother's memorial service, attended only by her husband, her three children, my sister-in-law, and my three daughters, my brother delivered her eulogy.

CHAPTER 19

∼

Situation Normal

I DID NOT SPEND MUCH TIME with my mother during the six months between her diagnosis and death. There were reasons for that. Not good reasons, just ones that I rationalized as acceptable, given my way of filtering the world and family dynamics, especially those between my mother and father at the time. It seemed perfectly normal that I wasn't visiting frequently or staying longer than two or three days when I did.

I told myself that we reacted to death differently than others. My father was a military man. We were a military family. From the time I was ten or eleven until I was twenty-two—the Vietnam years—someone's death had been a regular occurrence. At the height of it, when I was in high school, we'd see the green sedans carrying the bearers of the death notification traveling through our neighborhood. Our eyes would follow the car and conversations would stop momentarily as each of us thought about who we knew on that street. There was no morbid curiosity, no being drawn to the accident. We walked on. We'd know soon enough. And we were relieved when it wasn't our street or our house in front of which the sedan parked.

I lost friends from elementary and high school as well as college. My friends lost family members. I had witnessed death up close several times while directed through gory automobile accident scenes by police officers. I'd stood in the same rooms near the beds of dying patients and their family members while working as a crisis counselor and supporting my own client in the next bed in a small rural hospital with a three-bed emergency room. Sometimes the dying and their families were people I knew.

I listened as doctors and nurses in scrubs and masks rattled off numbers and followed procedures, then moved around each other in well-choreographed and practiced dances. Familiar to me were military funerals, the community coming together in ceremony to mourn and bury its own. Standing at attention. Flags. Salutes. Control.

My parents were not a short drive away. I worked at an extremely stressful job, often sixty hours a week, and there were still two children at home, one young enough to need more supervision and support than the other. Someone had to grocery shop, cook, and make sure she got to school and activities, which included almost weekly away competitions. And it was her senior year of high school. She took the required SATs and ACTs. We made college visits.

I continued to call my father to remind him that I could come out on weekends, take time off work, or come anytime they needed. I offered to make meals, give him a break, do any housework that needed doing. Or I could sit with Mom so he could nap or run errands.

"That's not necessary," he'd say. "We have a routine and your mother needs to rest. You have your children to take care of and your own responsibilities. The more normal things are the better. I'll call you if we need you."

I heard, "You'll just get in the way. You might upset your mother. We'll be fine."

I knew Dad did not think he needed me. But I wondered if my mother wondered why I didn't come. And though I knew I needed to see Mom, at some level, I was relieved my father waved me off. My mother knew I was exhausted. I could barely manage to keep my head above water in the rough sea that was my life as one wave after another knocked me down. It was getting harder and harder to get back up. I did not know how I could lose one or both of my parents, and I was worried about Dad's health too.

It had only been a year since a hospital social worker had said that my parents could no longer care for my paternal grandfather alone. Now at the age of 102, he lived in a nursing facility not too far away from their house, and I had hoped that they would reclaim their independence and freedom to live their retired life. Now this. I wanted to wail that it was unfair. But I didn't. Mom and Dad were not wailing or crying. How could I?

Adept at avoidance, I categorized my decision not to pack up the car and show up on their doorstep as respect for the two of them. They would let me know if they needed me. I did not consider what *I* needed; if I had, I would have admitted that I needed to be there.

Finally, I managed to get my mother on the phone, and asked if it would be okay if I drove out to visit that weekend. She said, "Of course! I'd love to see you."

Dad left me alone with Mom while he ran out for something at the store. It was impossible not to notice that she had lost a significant amount of weight. She asked if I minded helping her bathe.

"Of course not!" I said. "Let's do this."

"I can shower by myself," she told me, "but I just need help getting in and out of the tub."

She took off her robe, then turned to look at me, holding her bathrobe with two hands up to her neck. She paused before saying, "I am so embarrassed to have to ask you to do this."

"Mom," I responded, "If I were ill, would you do this for me?"

"Yes, of course I would," she told me, without hesitation. This seemed to make her feel better. Then she took off her nightgown and hung it on top of her robe on back of the bathroom door.

My mother had always been comfortable with her body, far more than I had ever been with my own. I'd always envied her for this. She had never been shy about taking off her clothes while dressing in front of me but seemed so now.

"Now don't be shocked," she said.

It was all that I could do not to gasp. I noticed the weight loss when I arrived, but I was not prepared to see skin and bones when she took off her nightgown. She looked like a malnourished twelve-year-old girl with no promise of a future.

I helped her into the tub and sat nearby while she washed herself and shampooed her hair. She approached showering—scrubbing her head and body—with so much effort that she reminded me of someone who'd just come out of the desert and jumped into a lake for the first time in a month. We didn't speak; I just watched, while giving her as much privacy as I could as I tried to make sure she did not lose her balance. It broke my heart.

"I don't like to ask your father to do this, you know."

"Why not, Mom?" I was surprised.

"I know he is willing, but you know your Dad. He's always in such a hurry. I don't want to feel rushed and I don't want him to lose patience with me."

I knew that this should be the farthest thing from my mother's thoughts. It just was not true. I watched my father care for my mother. After living with the news of the diagnosis for a few days, my mother had asked him, "You won't leave me alone, will you?" and he'd told her not to worry, of course he wouldn't. He gave up golf and anything else that wasn't related to her care. And though able to afford twenty-four-hour, in-home support for her given his wise choice of enrolling in extended-care insurance years before, he refused in the first few months to bring anyone in to help, choosing to do everything himself.

"Mom, just talk to him about it," I suggested. "I'm sure he isn't trying to rush you. He just moves a mile a minute, you know that. Tell him to slow down. I think it's hard for him."

My mother didn't respond.

That night, I made what I believe was my mother's last home-made meal—as Dad ordered out most nights and soon after she began a liquid diet.

Before leaving to return home, I wanted to set them up with some dinners they could reheat in the microwave, but I asked her what she wanted for dinner that evening. She said that she wanted pork roast with cabbage and apples.

"Now, brown the roast in the pan on all sides," she began as she told me how to prepare the meal.

"I've got it, Mom," I smiled at her. "You taught me how to make this meal."

"I did?" she asked.

I nodded. But then I realized that she wanted to be part of the preparation.

"I forget when I add the apples and cabbage," I told her.

She happily rattled off the instructions.

"Don't add any salt," she reminded me, "your father can't have any."

Later, when I brought a plate to her on a tray, she tasted it.

"This is delicious, Nancie." She finished it all.

It would be the last meal I ever saw her eat.

CHAPTER 20

Going Dark

THAT FEBRUARY, about three months after the diagnosis, while I traveled as one of the chaperones for Jane's Winter Color Guard Team, we were stranded in Peabody, Massachusetts, for two extra days after a weekend competition. In between supervising homework sessions, watching the kids make sleds out of cardboard boxes and duct tape while the wonderful hotel staff moved the snow they cleared in the parking lots into hills for them to slide down, and playing never-ending card games, I kept trying to call Mom and Dad to let them know where I was.

The first few times they didn't answer, I didn't worry. I knew my middle daughter, Sharon, would be out to visit, so I called when I knew she would be there. She had been a regular visitor during times I could not go, and Dad and Mom seemed more comfortable with her there than me. When she picked up the phone, I asked if everything was okay.

"Oh, you know," she tried to say casually. I sensed something was up.

"Can Mom or Dad come to the phone?" I asked her. She checked with Dad who told her they couldn't right then. I said I'd call back.

I tried calling several times after that. The first time, Sharon said that they were in the middle of something. The second time I called she said, "Grandpa says he can't come to the phone right now."

On my third attempt and her third reason for why they couldn't come to the phone, I used my mother's voice.

"Honey, tell your grandfather that I need to speak with him."

My father came to the phone that time.

"Hi, Nancie."

He sounded so tired. I had learned a long time ago that some people only answered questions they were asked and volunteered nothing else.

"Hi, Dad. How's Mom and what has changed since we last spoke?"

"Your mother is moving to hospice. I've gone over and chosen the place and the room. I wanted to make sure it was nice. She'll have a view of a lovely lake."

I didn't ask him anything else. Though I knew how I felt, I could not imagine how this was affecting him.

"I'll be home tonight Dad, and I'll drive out tomorrow."

"That will be good," he said. "Love you now."

When I spoke to Sharon next, I asked her how it was. She was especially close to my father, and somehow it seemed right that she was with him and Mom at that time.

I learned that she had been in the car driving out to their house when she got a call from Dad. He told her they were not at home, but at the hospital. She drove straight there, parked the car, and found the floor Mom's room was on. Dad was in the hallway standing outside my mother's room.

He filled her in. Mom had been unable to keep anything down and had some other frightening symptoms. When they called her doctor's office, they told Dad to take her to the hospital immediately. It wasn't too long after she was settled in a room that the doctor came in.

"Suzanne, I am so sorry. There is nothing else we can do."

They recommended hospice care, so Dad was just waiting for the transfer to take place when Sharon arrived at the hospital.

"She is not going to survive this," he told her.

"Grandpa's eyes teared up, so I told him that the allergens were really high," she revealed to me.

"What did he say?" I asked.

"'Yeah,'" she said. "That's all. Just 'yeah.'"

It occurs to me now that I don't remember talking to my children about much more than the logistics of Mom's care, my schedule of visits, the transportation schedules Rachel and Sharon would have to manage to make sure Jane made it to where she needed to go while I was away, and the daily reports on my mother's status after conversations with Dad. I have no memories of asking them how they felt, if they were sad, or afraid. I don't remember crying or telling them how I felt. I don't remember thinking that they might want to cry.

I understand now that by carrying on as though my mother's impending death was the most normal thing in the world, I put up a good front, thereby assuring that I did not fall into a canyon of emotions so deep I might not climb out again. I didn't speak to my father or my brothers about how I felt.

After all, Dad was on the frontlines. I just ran back and forth between there and my own home front when asked to. I didn't talk to my father or brothers about how I was feeling. I never asked how they were coping. I avoided exploring what my mother's impending death meant to me. I just tried to handle things and managed most of the time. But there were solitary moments in my pod at work when great waves of sadness and fear rolled from the soles of my feet through my body and the tears came.

It took many years for me to realize that though Mom and I did not talk directly about it, we each had known all along that she was dying, though Dad appeared not to believe it. He had not allowed himself to know until he stood outside Mom's room in the hospital, after the doctor said she recommended hospice care, that it was over. No matter how solid the strategy, no matter the planning, no matter how closely he followed the schedule for dispensing her medication, no matter how on time he was for all her appointments or how much time he spent with her trying to reassure her—Mom was going to die.

CHAPTER 21

~

Let it Come, As it Will

IN APRIL, two months after my mother began receiving hospice care, my father called me at home one night after work.

"I'd like to take you up on your offer to come out for a week or two," he said, "though I don't think it will be that long. The hospice nurse said it could be any day and that there is no reason your mom should have hung on this long."

I knew the reason. Mom had managed to live through her birthday, her granddaughter's and grandson's birthdays, and her fifty-fifth wedding anniversary. She was trying to hold on a little longer to get through Dad's birthday on May 2, which was a week away.

My middle brother, Jim, flew up from Florida. His wife would fly up later. Since my youngest brother, Clint, lived there already, my mother would have all her children at home when she died.

When I arrived, my father was tired, wan, and focused on Mom. He and Janet, her nurse, worked together like a well-oiled machine.

The day after my brother arrived from Florida, I ran into Dad coming out of his den. He said, "Listen, I've asked your brother to write your mother's eulogy. He'll do a good job. I can't do it."

I'd like to say that I focused on the feelings revealed in my father's statement "I can't do it" rather than the reaction I had. We'd never discussed it, but I planned to give my mother's eulogy. Clearly, she hadn't told him about our conversation. I felt passed over. But then I thought, I should have said something myself earlier. Now was not the time to say anything. I thought, "Okay." I rationalized away my disappointment.

Poor Dad. He wanted to give Mom's eulogy but is too sad.

My brother will do a great job. And he probably won't cry.

Dad doesn't know that Mom and I talked about this.

Who cares whether I give it or someone else. Mom just wanted to be remembered. I can help.

I found my brother at my father's desk.

"Are you working on Mom's eulogy?"

"Yes," he said.

"I'm happy to help. Do you need anything?"

"No, I think I'm good," he said, smiling at me before returning to the work.

I could not sort out my feelings. Everyone was sad. Not just me. Was this a girl/boy thing? Did my father think my brother was a better writer than I was? Mostly, why didn't I say something? I could have said, "I would like to say something, too." I didn't. And I was somehow more upset that—for my mother—I didn't stand up and assert myself. I'd made her a promise. But it was a promise that didn't really matter to her. She was going to be remembered. That's all she had wanted. And I knew my brother would do a wonderful job.

A day or so later, as I was walking through the house, I met Dad headed toward the kitchen.

"Did you want to say something at the service?" he asked.

"Yes, I would," I said.

"Okay. Your brother will go first."

I'd settle for that.

I thought about what I wanted to say. I was sure my brother would hit the high spots. I discussed it with the members of a close group of online writers I'd belonged to for years, since I updated them daily with the latest happenings. I let them know that I decided to read a poem. My mother loved poetry. It was not unusual for her to call and read something she'd written or read.

"Do you have time to listen to a poem?" she'd ask. I always did. "Don't you just love that?" she'd say. I loved her reading the poems to me more than some of the poems she chose to share.

I considered "Funeral Blues," by W. H. Auden, because my mother heard it for the first time when she saw *Four Weddings and a Funeral*.

"I loved that poem at the end of the movie," she told me. "I wonder who wrote it."

"Auden," I told her.

"Oh?" she said. "Do you think so?"

"Auden, Mom. W. H. Auden. Yes, I'm sure."

"That wouldn't be my choice," my friend, the poet Ruth Bavetta, wrote in the message board. "I've always liked this one."

She suggested "Let Evening Come," by Jane Kenyon, who wrote it while enduring the cancer that would take her own life. The images evoked of a farm as night falls were perfect. My mother came from a long line of farmers and visited the family farm in Ohio during summers after her family moved to New York when she was a child. But the last stanza comforted me and seemed perfect.

> Let it come, as it will, and don't
> be afraid. God does not leave us
> comfortless, so let evening come.

We settled in as a family for the first time in many years. It was good to have everyone there. Like myself, my brother worked during the times we weren't with Mom. Mom's nurse, Janet, was with her from about 9 A.M. until 3 P.M., so that Dad could rest, which he didn't, because he used that time to "keep the operation running." I spelled Janet and Dad when they needed help.

I made lunch and dinner, though sometimes we picked up meals from one of Dad's favorite local restaurants. I ran to the store when necessary. Dad ate early then went up to be with Mom for the rest of the night, taking over Janet's nursing duties.

During my shifts, I sat with my laptop on a small, Korean bed tucked into the bay window in her bedroom. I worked remotely, checking in at the office through email and chat messages. As it was a large room that ran the depth of the house, there was enough space for Dad to have positioned Mom's hospital bed diagonally between two windows at one end of the room, through which she had a view of the magnolia tree on her left and the large expanse of land partially screened by a crepe myrtle on her right. She'd been comfortable here for two and a half months. She moved in and out of consciousness now, sometimes clear of head, sometimes obviously somewhere else.

Sometimes, I caught a whiff of magnolia and forsythia from outside. Once I could have sworn I smelled roses, though there were none around my parents' home. It seemed ironic that it was spring, symbolic of hope, birth, and celebration. Promise and future. But this season both time and living were rooted in nothing but sadness and impending death.

It was always calm and quiet except for the light scratching of a random branch on the side of the house and my mother's and my breathing. Hers shallow and labored. Mine deep, my chest so tight that breathing hurt. My exhales were more sighs than breaths. I looked up frequently to see if I could still see her chest move. It became harder and harder. Sometimes I'd sit forward on the Korean bed and peer at Mom, and just as I might get up and walk across the room to her bed, I'd see her chest rise or a finger flutter imperceptibly.

The rest of the time, my fingers flexed, pointed, and reached, poised and ready, then dancing lightly across the keyboard. I tried to be quiet, but sometimes she would open one eye.

"Nancie? Is that you? Are you typing? You should rest," she'd say.

"I'm okay, Mom. You rest. Can I get you anything?"

She'd give me a look that floated on the spectrum between love and concern, leaving it to me to decide where it would land. Our eyes locked and I chose to believe that if she could smile, she would. We stared at one another for a moment. That moment became forever. Then she closed her eyes, while I returned to double duty. Work and waiting.

She was in such pain. Dad was meticulous about dispensing her pain medicine right on time, even when she fought him. He wanted there to be no chance it would wear off, exposing her to even a second of pain she did not have to feel. Sometimes I helped support her head. Her bones were loose inside her skin, she was so thin. I could have sworn I heard them rattle.

There were times she hallucinated. One day she called out to me.

"Nancie! Why are they here?"

"Where, Mom? Who do you see?"

She motioned weakly to the foot of her bed. "There. Why are *they* here?"

Another time, while Dad and Janet were trying to give her medicine, she cried out in a voice I did not recognize—so different from her own, which was always clear, precise, and correct. It seemed a country accent, rough and ungrammatical. For some reason, I suspected it was her grandmother's. And it was weak, aged, and feeble sounding.

"Don't give me any liquor now. I can't have no liquor."

I sat one morning and watched her for about a half hour. I suddenly wished I had the power to breath deeply enough, even while sitting across the room as I was, to suck the air out of her lungs—slowly, easily, in one long breath—so that I could remove all her pain and she could let go.

Janet let us know that she'd gotten permission to work over the weekend because, she said, "I'm sure your Mom will not make it beyond Sunday."

But Mom did. And because Janet had worked the weekend, she was required to take Monday and Tuesday off. A relief nurse came to fill in. She was nursing student and clearly inexperienced

and uncomfortable. But we were there and knew what to do, so I
didn't worry.

On Tuesday, I was in the room while the new nurse took her
lunch break. Suddenly Mom spoke clearly and in a stronger voice
than I'd heard for days.

"Oh, have you come to get me?"

I went over to her bed.

"Mom? Do you need anything?"

Her hands, colder than they'd been before, look mottled.
Her system was shutting down and her circulation slowing. Her
breathing was labored. I knew it would be soon. The visiting hospice nurse came soon after lunch and confirmed what I thought.

"It will be soon," she said. I heard her talking to Dad. It sounded
as though she was giving him instructions.

About an hour or so later, I heard familiar sounds. The relief
nurse and I stood up at the same time and moved toward Mom's
bed. I stood to Mom's left side, took her hand, and leaned down
close to her ear, "I'm here Mom. We're getting Dad."

The poor novice nurse stood away from the bed staring at my
mother.

"Give me your stethoscope," I told her, "and please get my
brother, he's across the hall."

She nodded and ran across the hall to the guest bedroom. My
brother came to the door of the bedroom, I nodded, and he ran
down the stairs before I could finish saying, "It's time. Get Dad."

As I held her hand, I rested my head as close as I could to her
pillow. I whispered, "It's okay, Mom. Dad's coming."

My mother began to call out for my father, "Lowen? Lowen?
Where's Lowen."

My parents' house is old and solid. Sound doesn't travel, so I
do not believe my father could hear my mother calling, he just
knew she was, because he knew her. From the landing I heard
him, as he began running up the stairs, "I'm coming, Suzanne. I'm
coming. I'm here." He took her hand in his.

With my father on her right, me on her left, my brother at the
foot of the bed, my mother died. I heard my father talking to her,

but I don't know what he said. I don't know if he was standing or kneeling or if he looked at her face. I remember vaguely seeing my brother but don't remember his expression. Instead I focused on my mother, telling her how much I loved her and that she could go, we would be alright. And as she struggled, I remember saying, over and over, "It's okay, Mom. You can let go. We'll be fine. I promise."

I looked up at one point and took in the scene. Dad, Jim, the nurse with no name, and me. We stood together as a family, yet singular in our experience of Mom's passing.

It's a horrible thing to watch someone you love die. I felt my mother dying with my whole body. As she struggled to breathe so did I. I raised my head and looked into her eyes when I thought I heard her last breath. I now know exactly what "when life leaves the eyes" or "when the spirit leaves the body" means. I watched Mom's eyes dilate—as though they were spinning—and go still. I felt *her* leave. I closed her eyelids.

I knew she was gone, but I took the stethoscope and listened for a heartbeat, felt for a pulse on her neck, then looked at the clock to check the time.

"In case I forget," I said to the nurse, "remember the time." Then I handed back her stethoscope. I stood staring at my mother's body trying to understand why I felt differently than I had a few moments ago. She looked so tiny in the bed.

We were all quiet for a minute before my father stepped away from the bed. And then my father said, "I'm so glad she didn't die with her eyes open. It's horrible when that happens."

I said nothing, but my brother's expression must have indicated that Mom's eyes were open when she died, because I heard Dad say, "Who closed them?"

My father looked at me and said nothing. "We need to call your brother," he said. "I have to call the hospice nurse."

The hospice nurse arrived quickly, as she was at another patient's house not far away. She confirmed Mom's death, Dad called the funeral home, and the two of them began the process of recording and disposing of the morphine and other controlled substances. Everything happened quickly. I had hoped my brother Clint would arrive after the funeral hearse departed with Mom's body, but I watched out the window as he walked toward the house, dressed in the camouflage military uniform of the day, just as the men from the funeral home wheeled my mother's body from the house. I watched him look at the gurney, clench his jaw and walk bravely into the house.

Dad came into the room.

"Take your mother's clothes out of the closets and out of her dresser. I want everything out of here."

I looked at my brothers.

"Dad, that can wait. We can . . ."

"I don't want to have to look at her clothes," Dad said. "It's too much."

"What would you like me to do with them? Shall I put them in the attic? We can look through them later."

"I want them out of the house." He was so definite. "We can donate them to Goodwill, the Salvation Army. I don't care. I want them gone today."

"Shall I pick something out for her to wear?"

"I've already taken care of that. The funeral home is handling all that," he said as my brother, Jim, looked at me sympathetically, and nudged Dad towards the door.

Clint brought me a box of large, black garbage bags and I began to empty my mother's dresses, blouses, and slacks from her closet. Every piece of clothing reminded me of something, even if it was just how baggy it had looked on her during the last six months. As I filled the bags, Clint took them, two at a time out to the truck. Then when we were done, he drove everything my mother owned, except her jewelry, over to the Salvation Army. I was sad for myself, but sadder for him that he had that last chore.

I went to tell Dad that we were done with the room, but he and Jim were not there. They weren't outside either. I learned later that my brother had taken him over to the golf club to get a drink.

I called the girls to tell them that their grandmother was gone. I asked Rachel to take her sisters shopping for black dresses or pantsuits to wear to the service. Then I signed on to my computer to notify my office of my schedule.

There was one email notifying our group that, yet again, we had a new boss. There was also an email from the boss introducing himself and requesting that we speak briefly that afternoon and that he had called a staff meeting in the morning. I reached out to one of the people on my team and asked her to let him know that my mother had just died, so I could not speak to him this afternoon, but that I would call into the meeting the next day.

God bless him. He responded almost immediately by instant message, extending his sympathy, and saying, "I mean this in the nicest way. Please do not call into the meeting. Take this time to deal with your mother's death." I sat there and started to laugh.

It was my father's seventy-sixth birthday. My mother had just died. I had just cleaned all her belongings out of the closets and dressers in her room. All her toiletries from the bathroom. She'd been gone just over an hour. We mourned as individuals, not a family. And I had considered calling into a meeting the next morning. I was obviously insane. I went upstairs, sat in my mother's empty room, and cried for the first time in years. I cried for the loss of her. I cried for everything I'd never cried for before.

CHAPTER 22

Taps

THE GIRLS PICKED UP my brother Jim's wife, Jennifer, at Dulles Airport, and then they all drove out to join the rest of us at Dad's. A memorial service was set up for two days later. Mom would be interred at Arlington National Cemetery about a month later. Dad seemed to cheer up a bit with the girls there. Jim worked on Mom's eulogy, and I went shopping for something to wear to the memorial service. Somehow, along the way, despite knowing that Mom's death was imminent, I never bought anything to wear to her funeral.

On the day of the service, we went over to the funeral home. It was on the route I took when out shopping or running errands. When I saw people gathered and walking in or out to the parking lot, I wondered: Were they family? Mourners? Had a parent or a grandparent died? I wondered if those driving by asked the same questions as they saw our small group parading through the doors.

We all marched into the large room where Mom's service was to be held. It wasn't just large; it was *huge,* with rows and rows of chairs. We would barely fill the front row—on one side. When I saw that Dad had chosen an open casket, I turned around to prepare Jane, as I knew she would have a hard time, and bumped into my sister-in-law, who was standing beside her, the two of them rigid and wide-eyed. As I'd anticipated, they were not comfortable with the open casket.

Jennifer whispered, "I don't think I can bear to see your mother in a casket. I don't want to remember her that way."

"It's okay," I told her, "you don't have to go up to the casket. You can just sit in the front row."

"I can't, Mom, I can't; I can't be that close," Jane cried.

"Okay, sit back a little where you're comfortable," I said.

"I'll stay with her," Jennifer said.

Later, when I turned around, I saw them sitting about twenty rows back, right up against the wall.

I walked up to the casket to see Mom and my head snapped back.

"Oh, Mommy," I said.

The funeral home's makeup artist had applied the pinkest lipstick to Mom's lips—a shade I would compare to Beach Blanket Pink. Jim walked up beside me, "What's wrong?" I tilted my head toward Mom. He looked down, then back up at me.

"Wow. I don't think I ever saw Mom wear pink lipstick," he said. "I don't think I ever saw her wear pink either."

"You certainly did not," I replied. Had any cosmetics been available and if I could have distracted Dad, I'd have redone Mom's makeup. My mother's makeup was always impeccable.

"It should be," Dad would say. "She takes long enough to put it on."

Dad came up to us and said, "They did a good job, didn't they?" We agreed.

Then he nodded his head to the back of the room where Jennifer and Jane sat crying together as far away from the casket as possible.

"Look at those two," he said. "Some soldiers they are. But I understand. It's hard."

Every now and then, Jim and I would look at one another—
no expression, no words. Just an acknowledgment. It broke the
tension and comforted me a bit. I looked at my brother Clint, his
bearing solid and respectful, and wondered how he felt.

Jim delivered a beautiful eulogy. It struck me that his was
so personal, drawing on specific experiences he'd shared with
Mom, while connecting all of us in remembering who she was.
It conveyed how well he knew her, too. How close they'd been.
He remembered that she'd liked Auden's "Funeral Blues," as he
did. He told of her going back to the theater and talking the ticket
taker into letting her in just long enough to see the screen credits
scroll so she could see the name of the poem and who wrote it.

I thought, *W. H. Auden, Mom. I told you. W. H. Auden wrote
"Funeral Blues."* I couldn't help it—I smiled.

As he spoke, there were times he appeared to be overcome, but
he'd pause, then continue without incident. When he was done, I
stood up and moved to the front to read Kenyon's poem.

I made it about three-quarters through the reading before I
choked up and began to cry. I hung my head and tried to catch my
breath. Mortified that I might not be able to continue, I stopped
for a few seconds then managed to finish.

After, a minister completed the service, and we left.

"Let's get something to eat," Dad said. Someone suggested the
Olive Garden, so we went there. We were seated quickly, the only
ones in the place dressed in suits and dresses. The server noticed.

"You all look nice," he said. "You're all dressed up."

I caught my brother's eye and saw he had the same thought
I did. We willed the server not to ask the next question—to no
avail.

"And where have you all been?"

Everyone at the table stopped talking, horrified, as my father
looked at the young man, paused, and then said, "To a funeral.
My wife's funeral."

"I'm never going there again," Dad said when we left the

restaurant. It would take fourteen years before he returned. I'm kind of sorry. I always liked their salad.

Due to the number of burials at Arlington Cemetery, the internment couldn't happen right away. About a month later, the day finally came.

~

I'd visited before, of course; not just as a tourist, but when my Uncle Bill was buried there, and when my second husband proposed to me near General "Blackjack" Pershing's grave twenty-three years earlier.

"Let's go off campus for lunch," he said. "It's a beautiful day for Arlington Cemetery."

I thought, *Arlington Cemetery? In the heat of summer?* I knew he was a history buff, and he loved Washington, DC. Besides, it would be a change from our usual lunch at The Tombs in Georgetown, so I said, "Okay."

A marriage proposal was the last thing on my mind that day as we trudged in office clothes through the cemetery. He seemed more purposeful, albeit a little on edge, but I thought it was because he was trying to follow the map. We stood at the head of General Pershing's grave, and he pointed toward the panorama of the city before us.

"This is one of the most beautiful views of Washington," he said, and I had to agree. Then he proposed. I accepted.

"Of all the places in this town, why here?" I asked him.

"Because our children and their children can always find the place where I proposed to you," he said. "Where our family started." I thought that was thoughtful and beautiful. I still do.

~

Now I was back to bury my mother, having not yet buried all my feelings about the marriage that had ended almost ten years before. The irony of a marriage proposal in a cemetery didn't hit me until then. I imagined my mother looking over at me, at first expressionless to gauge what I was thinking, then in recognition, grinning with conspiratorial mischief. I had to smile to myself.

On this sad day I took more notice of things I had not paid as much attention to before. Other people with cameras walking. The quiet surrounding me, despite the crowds. Others standing or sitting through their own loved one's graveside service. The periodic wail of a bugler playing taps.

First, we arrived at a small building reserved for gathering and meeting with a chaplain before moving as a group to the gravesite. Other families met with the chaplain assigned to them by branch of service. Our chaplain was wonderful. What a job he had. He asked questions about Mom and encouraged us to tell him anything we thought important.

Dad had many things to share. 'Oh, she always said she wanted to be carried to her grave by six good-looking soldiers,' he told the chaplain at one point.

The size of Mom's memorial service at the funeral home may have been small, but her interment was not. We had expected just our immediate family, but slowly the meeting place filled up. My first husband and his wife came, my second husband attended, friends of the girls, friends and neighbors of mine, and people from my office. Our group slowly grew. I was surprised and deeply moved. When it was time, everyone lined up in their cars as instructed, and convoyed over to the gravesite.

As we drove up, I saw the hearse and seven tall, good-looking soldiers in dress blues, standing by.

The chaplain explained to all of us gathered there, "Suzanne wanted six good-looking pallbearers. We brought an extra in case one fell out."

My eyes turned from them to the gravesite where I saw some chairs and people beginning fill the lawn behind them. Mom would be leading a column. The last on her row. The latest to arrive. I heard my father say, "Damn, she's going to hate that. Hell, I'm going to hate it." Someday he, too, would be buried there.

"Hate what, Dad?" I asked.

He pointed to our left. Across the way loomed the Pentagon, or what my father referred to as Fort Fumble. He had hated the time he was stationed there.

When the time comes and Dad is buried with Mom, his casket will move to the graveside on a horse-drawn caisson. He'll receive the twenty-one-gun salute and a bugler playing "Taps"—one of the saddest sounds I've ever heard. As a military wife who served by standing and waiting, my mother was not entitled to any of that, of course. But the chaplain acknowledged her service by reading the words to "Taps."

I remember being tearful and beginning to quake from my chest. Not tremble—*quake*. I felt someone touching me, gentle and firm. When I looked, I saw the hands of my youngest daughter, her hands placed on my shoulders, looking at me. She smiled reassurance. Her two sisters stood at her side nodded and smiled at me as well. Giving me strength.

PART V

A person's identity is not to be found in behaviour, nor—important though this is—in the reactions of others, but in the capacity to keep a particular narrative going. The individual's biography, if she is to maintain regular interaction with others in the day-to-day world, cannot be wholly fictive. It must continually integrate events which occur in the external world, and sort them into the ongoing 'story' about the self.

—Anthony Giddens

CHAPTER 23

~

Relata Refero: *All the Stories*

U P UNTIL THE AGE OF FOUR, I spent much my life in my
great-grandparents' home, and I complied with the edict
of being seen and not heard. As a little girl, it was easy
to become invisible. During the day, adults were sometimes
unaware or even forgot that I played nearby. Some nights after I
was put to bed, sounds from the large kitchen in the back of the
house beckoned to me. In my footed pajamas, I crept down the
steep stairs—always careful to avoid that one stair Grandma told
me about, the one that Uncle Jack used to avoid when he snuck
in late, because it squeaked—from the middle bedroom on the
second floor to the landing in front of the swinging door into the
kitchen. I could push it open just enough to peek in.

The big kitchen I knew during the day, bright with sunlight
and filled only with sounds from the radio and my grandmother's
voice as she prepared meals, folded laundry, or sipped tea,
changed with the absence of daylight. The air in the room seemed
thick, mixed with cigarette smoke, and the light from the ceiling
lamp appeared yellow. The people were different, too. My grandmother's apron was gone. She sat at the kitchen table with other

women—sometimes my aunts, her friends, or my grandfather's cousins. The women wore jewelry and lipstick, and they'd done their hair.

The men wore the same white shirts they'd worn to the office that day, with collars open, no ties, and rolled up sleeves. They leaned against the counters or the stove, cigarettes in one hand and tumblers of scotch or bourbon in the other.

And as I listened to my relatives and their friends discuss, brag, and gossip from my place on the landing at night or from the corner in the kitchen where I played in the mornings, I witnessed how a story told one day, whether it was true or not, morphed, epic in its retelling, as it passed from one person to another—a day, a week, a year, one generation to another—until codified in our family's history and, ultimately, in my sense of self.

~

More than five years had passed since I first moved in with Dad before I learned that my father's uncle Al Murphy had not been a polygamist after all. And, contrary to family lore, not one of his three wives had been Chinese. I was both shocked and disappointed.

"Everyone knew Al," I'd been told. Relatives described Uncle Al, though not a tall man, as very strong and physically fit, a tough cop who walked a beat in Brooklyn where he'd grown up as one of John Valentine (Pop) and Anna Marie (Nana) Murphy's five children—Margaret, Al, my grandmother Eleanor, Harry, and Grace.

I do not remember meeting Uncle Al, though he didn't die until I was twenty. I don't even remember hearing that he'd died. But I felt I knew him well. My mental picture of him had been drawn by the words I'd heard in relatives' discussions about him during short and infrequent visits my family made to Brooklyn between moves from one military station to another. In my mind, he was muscular, with a dark head of hair, unlike his light-haired siblings. I pictured him as stern and serious looking. He stood on the sidelines or in the shadows of my imagination, his gaze penetrating. Perhaps I'd seen a photograph of him. He seemed as real to me as if he'd been present during those times I lived with or visited my grandparents.

I knew from stories my father told me that he felt close to his uncle as a child. He believed their special relationship was forged during the time Al, in between marriages, stayed for two years in the bedroom my father shared with his older brother Jack. Dad's oldest brother, Bill, was away in the Army Air Corps. This left one empty bed in the middle room on the second floor. Al slept there.

My father described his uncle as quiet and observant. "He was more of a listener than a talker, unlike others in the family," Dad recounted with a glance at me. "He didn't say much. He just watched and listened." Those who know my father might think the same of him.

"Every now and then, Uncle Al would do something to irritate my father on purpose," Dad told me, "like pour his coffee from his cup into the saucer and slurp it down. We knew he was daring my father to say something, but my father never did."

Dad went on, "You know, not long before my father died, he told me that he had feared Al. This surprised me. I wouldn't have expected that. To me, he was always Uncle Al. My roommate."

My father shared that Al took him under his wing. He even taught my father to box after watching Dad get pummeled by his brother Jack.

"One day Al said, 'Come here, Lowen.' Then he took me downstairs to the basement where he had set up a boxing ring. He handed me some gloves and taught me all the moves. And after a few training sessions, when Jack came at me again, I beat the hell out of him." Dad looked at me with a satisfied smile. "Al laughed, and Jack wasn't happy." Al and Jack did not get along.

"Al could be a fighter," Dad revealed one day as we drank tea in front of the television in his den. "One night, when Al and I were at the kitchen table, Pop came home from Charlie's Delicatessen with a black eye. He was holding his head and had a huge bruise on his forehead. You could tell his nose had been bleeding." Dad said.

Dad took some time to explain that Charlie was Pop's friend and served the best beer in the neighborhood. Then he went on, "When Pop walked in and we saw that he was hurt, Al asked him, 'What happened, Pop?'"

"Nothing." Pop replied.

"Pop, what happened?"

Pop told Al that some guy hanging out with Harold and Tommy, the Burke twins, had punched him in the face.

Dad said, "Al got quiet. Then he wiped his mouth with his napkin, got up from the table and said, 'I'll be right back.'"

My father laughed and shook his head as he remembered.

"Charlie told us he warned the man who punched Pop to leave before Al found out what he'd done and came over to the bar, but the guy said he wasn't going anywhere and asked, 'Who the hell is Al?' Just about that time, Al came through the door and Charlie pointed at him: 'That's Al.'"

"Al walked up to the guy, and asked, 'Did you punch my father?'"

According to Dad, based on the accounts of unidentified witnesses at the scene, "Before the man could open his mouth, Al decked him with one punch. He just laid him out flat. Then he stood over him and said, 'If you ever hit my father again, I'll kill you,' and walked back out the door."

"Charlie was very relieved that it was Al who came to handle things because it was fast and over with one punch. That bum was out cold and nothing else in the place was damaged."

Stories about the fighting men in our family were plentiful. Some told of gallantry, chivalry, or events where someone found himself in the wrong place at the wrong time. But my favorite Uncle Al story did not involve a fistfight.

~

After World War II, my Uncle Bill left the Army Air Corps for a short time and took a job as a pilot for one of the big oil companies. He flew to and from the Middle East.

As told to me, Bill walked into a dark, smoke-filled speakeasy in Saudi Arabia one night and found Uncle Al sitting on a crate playing poker and—this is important—wearing a fez. I was fascinated by the fez. I liked that word the first time I heard it. The sound of it. *Fez.* I liked the look of it, too, when they showed me a picture of what a fez was. Red with a gold tassel. To this day, the word fez conjures up an image I once saw of the actor Peter Lorre.

"Al?" Bill squinted his eyes and looked across the room. "What are you doing here?"

"Bill! Pull up a chair," Al called out, as though it were the most natural thing in the world for his nephew to walk into that joint just at that time. He chomped on his cigar, swigged some beer, then kicked a free crate toward my uncle, who sat down at the makeshift table. Al handed Bill a beer and he joined the game, too. They stayed up all night playing poker and catching up.

"Well, that part might have been true," my father thought out loud the afternoon I asked him about that story as we sat drinking our afternoon tea.

"They told me that Uncle Al left Brooklyn in a hurry because the three women he was married to at the same time found out about one another," I said.

"He was *not* married to all of them at the same time." My father shook his head. "He was married three times but *not* at the same time. You could make good money in Saudi Arabia then. Maybe Al had alimony to pay and he had children to support."

"Did you know his wives?" I asked.

"Yes. They were all lovely women. I knew one of his children, my cousin Jackie. She was a little girl then. I was a teenager. I used to carry her around on my shoulders. His first wife was my favorite though, because I knew her best and she was my godmother. I thought she was beautiful."

"Was she the Chinese wife?" I asked. I did not know much about her.

"*Chinese wife?*" My father turned away from the television and stared at me in disbelief. "Where did you get that idea?"

"Grandma, Grandpa, Uncle Bill, others. . . . Someone told me that his first wife was Chinese."

"No. She was *not* Chinese." He thought for a while, then said, "She had black hair. She had one of those haircuts, you know, like the roaring twenties. Short with bangs." He waved his hands and wiggled his fingers around his head.

"A bob?"

He nodded and stared at the television.

"Could she have been a flapper?"

"Maybe. Yes. I think she probably was."

Dad thought a moment. "She was small, very tiny. Always dressed in very stylish clothes. I remember her clothes. She was really sweet and nice to me. I loved her."

I'd always imagined Aunt Gladys in a traditional Chinese *qipao*. Maybe I'd seen a picture of her in a high-necked flapper sheath and just thought she was Chinese. Maybe Grandma told me her hair was cut like a Chinese doll. That's something my grandmother might have said. For a moment I accepted that I must have misunderstood the stories and just thought Al's first wife was Chinese.

No. I knew what had been said and what I'd overheard. I wasn't the only one who heard it. The story *always* popped up in the routine of any family gathering, no matter the size of the group or who was there.

"You know, Al, Eleanor's brother? He was married to three women at the same time. One was Chinese. He had to get out of Brooklyn when they found out about each other. Bill found him hiding out in Saudi Arabia wearing a fez."

No one had ever stopped that day's oral historian to say, "What are you talking about? That's not true." Instead, they nodded and laughed no matter how many times they heard it or who told the story.

~

"Why would they make up a story like that about Uncle Al?" I asked Dad.

"Because they were bullshit artists, all of them. That's why," Dad said.

I took a quick inventory of the best stories I'd been told me through the years. I'd loved and devoured them. Knowing them made me feel part of the family, no matter where I was or how long I'd been gone. Upon my return, my ability to start on the same page as everyone else proved, at least to me, that I belonged there as much as I imagined my cousins did. And whenever I returned home after being away, I interviewed, listened, and catalogued any new stories that I might have missed or events that might have occurred while I was away.

The stories became part of me. They shaped my idea of who I was and where I'd come from. They served as the familiar while my family moved from state to state, country to country, far away from "home." I relied on the stories to make my ordinary family seem extraordinary, if only in my own mind, when I felt the need.

Based on who told it, when I had heard it, and how I interpreted it, a story might support the reasons for life decisions I'd made. Now these stories became suspect. Which ones weren't true? Which ones were? And why had they been so important to me? Now I felt as though I had been caught in a lie. Many lies. As though I'd made them all up myself.

I wondered why I had loved the myth of Uncle Al so much. Maybe I'd needed to believe that no matter how far away we were from home, we didn't change, and neither did those we left behind. Maybe the story reinforced a wish that no matter where in the world we were, we might bump into friends and family. They'd remember us and be happy to see us. That story made the world seem small and the distance between where I was at any given time and where I believed I was from shorter. Polygamy and Asian influences sprinkled throughout were just seasoning.

Dad continued to watch his televised poker game. Men in sunglasses and baseball caps sat around a game table as they stared at their cards, fiddled with poker chips, and considered their next moves. I was sad for Uncle Al. Clearly Dad had loved him. At some point so had three women and his children. He'd been a policeman, a good uncle, a family man to many—but he'd been remembered as someone he wasn't.

~

Someone in the televised poker game folds, and they break for commercial. Dad stands up.

"I'm getting another cookie," he says, and heads toward the kitchen.

I get up to follow him while I continue to think about all the stories that make up our family canon. I want to ponder how family stories heard through childhood filters, coupled with lack of life experience and context, create misunderstandings and shape the adult a child becomes. And I can't help but search for some truth in the one about Uncle Al.

"Hey, Dad." I speak to his back as he walks out of the room, and I try to keep up with him.

"What about the fez? Do you think Uncle Al really wore a fez?"

"Oh, I'm sure of it," Dad says.

CHAPTER 24

~

Driving Issues

MY FATHER TOOK POSSESSION of his father's Florida driver's license and his car keys when Grandpa was almost one hundred years old. Dad had taken Grandpa to the ophthalmologist who told my grandfather, "Absolutely no more driving. You can't see." I don't know why it took them that long to make that determination. Fifteen years prior I took three-year-old Rachel down for a visit. Grandpa nearly killed us by running through several intersections in a row on our way to Kroger's.

"OH MY GOD! WE'RE GOING TO DIE!" I screamed.

"What's the problem? Calm down," my grandfather told me.

"Grandpa, you just ran through three intersections without stopping."

"Well, who can concentrate when you're screaming like a banshee?" he retorted.

I did not get into the car with him for the remainder of my visit. If we needed something, I snuck out while he was in the bathroom so he couldn't offer to drive me.

"Go! Go!" my grandmother would whisper, watching the hallway as I grabbed my daughter and ran for the front door. "He's still in there. He'll be there forever."

As they left the doctor's office, Grandpa pulled his spare set of car keys out of his pocket and headed for the driver's side of his car.

"Oh, no you don't, Dad," my father said. "Give me those keys."

And Grandpa didn't drive again. Not too long after, my grandmother died, and Dad brought Grandpa up to live with him and Mom.

In the original script that I wrote about my life with Dad, he comes to me one morning and says, "Here are my car keys. It's time I stop driving." Another unanticipated plot twist—I don't think that's going to happen. First, I've determined that it's against human nature for any human being who has a license to give it up willingly. Second, my father doesn't think I'm a good driver. Third, my father thinks he still is.

Dad was always a good, defensive driver. He taught me to drive because while he was in Vietnam and all my friends were taking drivers ed, my mom refused to let me.

"What if you get into an accident?" she'd say. "We only have one car."

Finally, to stop my begging, she said, "Listen, just stop bothering me about that. Since I'm not ever going to let you drive anyway, there's no need for you to have a license."

By the time I was seventeen, Virginia changed the law to state that anyone under eighteen had to have taken drivers ed. With all our moves, I hadn't. I've always thanked Virginia's politicians for legislating that I get my license; but actually, it was about money. Drivers ed would have been free if I'd taken it in school. Now Mom and Dad would have to pay for a private instructor. Dad said he'd teach me to drive.

There were a few rules. First, I had to learn to drive a stick shift. Second, I had to wear my seat belt. Third, he didn't have to.

"Will you put on your seat belt, Dad?" I asked politely and

responsibly after taking my seat behind the wheel, inspecting the dashboard, and adjusting all the mirrors and before starting the ignition.

"I'm not wearing one," he said as he puffed on his pipe. "I need to be able to jump if necessary."

It didn't take me too long to learn to drive the Volkswagen Beetle Dad used to commute, though shifting and clutching in the right way did. Finally, Dad decided I could try the station wagon. I climbed behind the wheel, Dad rode shotgun, and Mom sat in the back seat with my brothers. I pulled the car out of our little street and navigated carefully along our neighborhood roads. There wasn't a lot of space because it was after work and the street was lined with parked cars. Trying hard not to hit anything, I sped up a little, at which point my mother began to scream, "She's going to kill us all. Stop her, stop her!"

"Mom!" I said as I looked in the rearview mirror. Her face was pale, and she had my brother in a bear hug pressed up against her. It made me so nervous that I stopped the car. Dad told me to switch seats with Mom.

I never drove the station wagon again and never had another driving lesson, but before the deadline of my eighteenth birthday, Dad said my friend Francis could take me down to get my license. As we drove away, I looked back at the house through the rearview mirror. My mother was standing on the front lawn, hands clenched to her bosom as though she'd never see me (or the car) again.

I passed my written test and had no problem with the driving part, either, but as we left, I let out a "Whoop!" and proceeded to run through a four-way stop. Francis didn't bat an eye.

My parents let me drive from then on, but I knew that any infractions and my driving privileges would be revoked.

～

Shortly after I "earned" my Virginia driver's license, we moved to North Carolina. This happened in the last six weeks of my senior year of high school while my father was stationed at Fort Bragg. Perhaps to ease the pain of not graduating with my friends in Virginia, they let me drive our Volkswagen Bug to school almost every day.

One day Dad came home unexpectedly for lunch. "This can't be good," I said to myself.

"I want to talk to you," he said as he walked through the door into the kitchen. Then he leaned back casually, arms outstretched, against the kitchen counter. Crossing his feet at the ankles he looked at me. Despite his casual positioning, I tensed a little in my chair at the kitchen table. From his expression and his posture, it appeared as though this might not be too bad. Yet his combat boots and battle fatigues gave him an edge. You just never knew. It might be a trick, a surprise attack.

"You were observed driving ninety miles an hour toward Post this week after school," he said, staring into my eyes.

I accepted the challenge and held his gaze—I had practiced staring back without blinking a lot—while I asked, "What day? What time?" and searched my memory for when this could possibly have happened.

"It doesn't matter what day. After school you're supposed to head straight home, and you are supposed to keep to the speed limit. He said you were driving like a maniac. Are you trying to kill yourself or someone else?"

"Who said this?"

"It doesn't matter. You don't know him."

You might ask how someone I didn't know knew me or that I was my father's daughter. Whether on a military base or "on the economy" nearby, anyone military or from a military family could know who you are, especially if your father was a battalion commander. Military communities are villages—incestuous villages. Also, back then, all automobiles belonging to military personnel had stickers that identified to whom they belonged, including their rank. These were required for entry through the main gates and onto the Post. How many battalion commanders could there be with a robin's egg blue Volkswagen Beetle and an eighteen-year-old daughter on Fort Bragg?

"How could he know how fast anyone is going?"

"He clocked you."

"How? Is he an MP?"

"Never mind about that. He said you were speeding." Dad was losing patience.

"But Dad, I could not have driven ninety miles an hour. At that speed, the doors and tires would fall off the Bug. If I was speeding at all it was maybe, at most, ten miles an hour over the limit." Damn. I'd just admitted to speeding. Something made me wonder if he'd said "ninety miles an hour" to trick me into admitting I'd been speeding after all.

"Anything over the speed limit is unacceptable! Is that clear? If you can't obey the speed limit and I hear anything else about speeding, you will not drive. Understood?"

"Yes, sir."

That time I was innocent—of speeding. I had not been on that road after school at that time that whole week. Instead, I'd taken a few detours and made stops at other places each day after school. For instance, one day I'd taken a couple of girlfriends over to Methodist College to watch a baseball game because my boyfriend at the time was the pitcher for the visiting team from Elon College. I did a quick analysis.

I'd already been counseled about coming straight home from school unless I had permission not to, so I faced possible loss of driving privileges. I evaluated my defense options. What did I do? I copped to speeding, a first-time offense. As my father taught me, one must choose her battles.

I want to make clear that my father was not the Great Santini or anything like the stereotypical military mean man portrayed in too many books and movies. I also want to stress that most of the fathers of other military brats I knew were not. He wasn't a hothead. His expectations were not unfair, and his punishments were not physical. There were rules. He made sure we knew them.

It was up to us to follow them or accept responsibility for not doing so.

I seldom saw him act in anger or raise his voice. He meted out punishment relative to the crime. For my brothers and me, Dad's displeasure or disappointment was the worst penalty. What he thought of me mattered more than anyone else's opinion. In my heart and mind, Dad held the highest rank in my chain of command.

~

I can count on one hand the number of times he has let me drive if he's going to be in the car with me. Two times I was driving him to the hospital. The other two were when I followed him to drop off his car at the mechanic and had to drive him home and back when his car was ready. I fully expected him to ask me for my keys. But I guess he figured it would be silly to ask me for the keys to my own car so he could drive it. Most of the time he gets around this problem by asking the FOGs to take him.

There have been a few incidents when he's been distracted or tired. He'll drive a little too close to the center lane or off on the shoulder. I've learned not to scream, but I ride defensively keeping my eye one the road, watching for other drivers and making sure to point out things that might be a problem.

One night in the car, I was fiddling with my phone and heard him start to laugh.

"What's so funny?" I asked him.

"We were almost killed at that intersection. There was no screaming so I thought you might be in shock."

"What did you do?" I asked.

"Nothing! Why do you always think I did something?"

I've gotten better at not screaming. I've decided that it won't do me a bit of good and might make things worse. One night, Dad and I went out a little later than we realized. Not only did it turn dark on our way home, but we got caught in a torrential downpour. Visibility was nil except for the flashing police and ambulance lights we saw in the distance just short of our house.

"I'm going to take a detour," Dad said, "I'll turn around up here."

Thinking he meant into the parking lot of The Dollar Store a few yards up, I said, "Good idea," but Dad started to take an immediate hard left right in the middle of the road.

"Jesus, Dad!" I yelled.

"What? I'm just going to go into the parking lot here and turn around," he said.

"There's no driveway, Dad," I was not yelling.

THUMP

"Oh. This is bad," he said as cars headed toward our stalled SUV standing horizontal across the road (with me on the side they'd hit, I might add). "You know it's hard for some people to see in the dark and with this weather . . . people like me," and he started laughing. I did not join him.

I continue to be watchful and to prepare myself for the fact that it may well require, despite all my hope otherwise, my brothers and me to push Dad to hand over the car keys. Taking the car keys is not a hill I choose to die on alone. I know I am better prepared to have that difficult conversation now than I would have been previously. Yet I continue to hope that Dad's typical awareness and common sense will prevail and that I won't have to rewrite that part of my original script.

CHAPTER 25

~

Medical Advisory Team

*A*FTER ABOUT FOUR YEARS of living with Dad, I settled in, and Dad seemed used to my being there. I responded well to the imposed structure of his life. We fell into a regular pattern and continued to share stories and experiences, gaining new perspectives about one another and others in our family, as well as people we have known.

I appreciate that it has not always been this way, that it wasn't always easy. One of the hardest areas has been around matters of health. For the most part, Dad is an excellent patient. He has regular doctor and dentist appointments. He keeps them. He follows whatever he is told to do and, thank heavens, I think he lucked into a fantastic team of doctors—primary physician, cardiologist, and dermatologist.

When he comes back, I always ask what the doctor said. He always gives me vague answers. "No change." Or "I'm doing great for someone who's in his eighties." I interpret this as he didn't ask any questions, or he doesn't want to tell me. When the doctor changes a course of treatment or a prescription, I ask if the doctor told him why.

"Hell, no," he tells me.

"Dad, did you ask?"

"Why do I need to ask him? He's the only one who needs to know why. I just do what he tells me."

He does know what all his pills are for, though not always which pill is for which "thing."

One night I asked him if he had any antacids. He said, "Oh, I have a pill for that. Take it for a few days and see if it works. I have tons of these."

I was in so much pain, I figured it wouldn't hurt to take one or two until I got to the doctor myself. I looked at the bottle. I didn't recognize the name, but it said to take one a day. I figured that wouldn't kill me. I'd take one for the evening and then call the doctor's office in the morning.

"Is this generic, Dad?"

"What? Oh, yeah."

About thirty minutes later it occurred to me to look the pill up. I pulled up a browser and searched.

"Dad! This isn't an antacid. This is for hypertension and angina."

"Oh. Well, I'm pretty sure you have hypertension, and no one wants angina, believe me."

I begin to look at his medications and research what they were for. Then I went to the pharmacy and got two more pillboxes, each for a week's worth of pills.

I held up the new pillboxes and said, "Dad, I got you two extra pill boxes. I can fill them up for you so that you always have at least two more ready to go."

"Sounds good," he said.

Not too long after that conversation I went away for a week. On the drive back from the airport, just as I crossed the bridge, I called as I always did. He didn't sound good.

"I've been sick."

"I can hear that, Dad. You sound croupy and weak. Have you been to the doctor?"

"No, if I don't get better, I'll go."

He hadn't been feeling well for the week before I left and had promised to go if things didn't get better. I calculated that this was headed into his third week. He sounded so ill that I said, "Dad, when I get home, we're going to the emergency room."

"No, we're not," he said. "I'll call the doctor tomorrow."

"It's Memorial Day tomorrow," I said.

"Oh. Well, I'll go Tuesday."

I didn't want to push him, so I waited until I got home.

When I saw Dad, he looked pale—almost gray. I felt his forehead.

"Dad, you have a fever, you're weak, and this has been going on too long. We're going to the emergency room."

"No, we're not," he said. "I'll call the doctor Tuesday."

I decided to try a tactic I used with my children.

"It's a holiday weekend, so it might be better not to go tonight. Let's go first thing in the morning. Early before anyone has any car accidents on their way home from the beach."

"That sounds liked a good idea," he said.

He went to bed that night and I stayed up to make sure he was okay. Just about the time I would head across the hall to see if he were breathing, I'd hear him cough so I knew he was still alive at least.

The next morning, I was sitting in the den when he came downstairs. He had showered, he was dressed, his hair was combed, and he was carrying his toiletry kit under his arm.

"Let's go. I'm ready. I think they'll probably keep me," he said.

I drove him over to the hospital. He was having a hard time breathing, and I could hear the fluid in his lungs as he sat next to me in the car. After we parked in the lot near the ER entrance, I walked ahead of him to open the door.

"Dad, I'm doing the talking. Don't say anything." He just looked at me.

I pushed open the door and a nurse looked up at me. "I have an eighty-seven-year-old man coming in. His pulse is thready and I hear fluid in his lungs."

The nurse came around the reception desk with a wheelchair. Dad didn't argue. He sat down. They took him right in. A nurse did a workup and the doctor on duty came in.

After X-rays, they concluded that Dad had a slight case of pneumonia but were more concerned about his vitals. His oxygen was low and his heartbeat irregular. They admitted him. I knew he felt extremely ill because he didn't argue. He was in good spirits, kidding around as usual, but put up no resistance to staying the night. I stayed with Dad until he was settled and learned that they would put him through a bunch of tests the next morning. I went home to let my brothers know and to call my girls.

My brother asked if he should catch a flight up and I said not to until we knew more from the tests.

I called my oldest daughter, Rachel, before I called her sisters.

"I'll be out as soon as I can," she said.

"Oh, honey, they'll be doing tests tomorrow. Why don't you wait and see what they say first . . .," but she interrupted me.

"Okay, but I'll be there the day after tomorrow. By midday," she insisted. I figured we'd have enough information by then.

I was grateful it was a holiday; it gave me time to get a few things done so that when I called into my office on Tuesday morning to say I'd be out for a day or two, no one would inherit too big a mess. Then I headed back to the hospital.

Dad was sitting up in bed. His vitals had not improved. I watched the monitor on his bed. The nurse explained that he was in congestive heart failure. I didn't hear her as she explained where they wanted his oxygen levels and heart rate to be. My countenance was calm. I felt myself nodding, but worried that I would faint. I remembered the last time I thought my father was dying.

～

It was a holiday weekend then, too. My father was at the U.S. Army War College in Carlisle, Pennsylvania, before leaving for Korea. I was up for a visit and reading the newspaper in the living room when my father came into the living room from outside.

He was clutching his chest. He was perspiring and looked ashen. Though calm, he fell onto the sofa and said, "Get an ambulance."

I ran to the phone in the kitchen, picked it up and said, "Get an ambulance over here. I think my father's having a heart attack!"

Then I hung up and looked at my father. I realized that I hadn't given them our address or my father's name.

"Good one," my father said.

I stood there immobilized and so panicked I didn't have the brainpower to remember to tell the ambulance where to go. Dad seemed more amused about it than worried though. In a moment I heard the ambulance.

"They know where every call on this post comes from," Dad said as though to answer my unasked question. They took him to the hospital in the ambulance, and by morning they determined it was a hiatal hernia, not a heart attack.

〜

I laughed a little as I thought how that episode added to the stories about my fear of blood. I was glad Rachel would be with me the next day.

Rachel arrived as promised and if I had any concerns that Dad would have the medical advocacy any patient needed, I stopped having them. I stood back and watched with wonder as she familiarized herself with the room, introduced herself to the nurses, and monitored what they did—and then I noticed her walk out to the desk.

"What were you telling them?" I asked when she returned.

"I gave them a "Post-it Note" with my name and cell phone number and let them know that they needed to call me about what was happening. I told them to put it right in his chart."

I looked over at my father. If I had done that, I was sure he'd have been annoyed. But he was totally fine with Rachel taking over. In fact, quite amused. Every now and then a nurse would ask him something and he would point to Rachel and say, "You'd better talk to her."

In no time, everyone began talking to Rachel along with Dad. I was so relieved.

I put Rachel on the phone when we called my brother. She spoke to her uncle and filled him in on everything. I marveled at how she had managed to collect so much more information that I would have felt comfortable or thought to ask for. Some kind of advocate I was.

We were there the next day when the cardiologist came in to see Dad. He informed us that Dad's heart was functioning at about 50 percent and that because of that, blood was pooling and they were concerned about clots. This precluded any of the procedures that might improve things for fear he would throw a clot and have a major stroke.

Rachel looked at the doctor. "So what options *are* possible?" she asked.

"Unfortunately, in this situation, there is nothing available that wouldn't put him at risk for a major heart attack or stroke," he told her. Then he looked at my father.

"We'll stabilize you, get your oxygen levels up. Maybe send you home with some oxygen."

I said nothing, but Rachel looked at the doctors and said firmly, but sweetly, "Oh. There has to be another option."

Then she looked at my father and said, "We'll get you stabilized, and then we're taking you across the bridge. We'll get a second opinion at the Heart Center at INOVA in Virginia. It's not far from my house, so it will be easy for us to get back and forth."

The doctor said nothing. My father said nothing. Rachel smiled a lovely smile at the doctor and said, "I've got to go make a call. I'll be back."

I walked over and sat by Dad's bed.

"If I need to have oxygen, it's over," he said.

I looked at him.

"I mean it. I can't play golf with a tank of oxygen."

I thought he was trying to joke, but when I looked at him, he was serious. He seemed to be telling me that if living required oxygen, his life was over.

I said something he used to say to me when I was a child, worried or afraid, and anticipating the worst: "Let's wait and see what happens, Dad." Then I added, "You can't go anywhere right now. I don't have a plan B." I laughed and he grinned at me. It was true. I couldn't bear for him to die. That was not part of my plan.

I went to look for Rachel. She was keeping in touch with her office and her family. We decided to grab a sandwich in the café.

"Look," she said, "if they are going to say there are no options, it doesn't hurt to get a second opinion."

"If he'll go along with it," I said.

"Oh, he'll go along with it," she mumbled with a mouth full of chicken salad. "He has no choice. We'll convince him."

After lunch, the doctor came back in. "There may be one thing we can try. We can use a camera and check to see if there are any clots present. If there are, it's no go. But if there aren't, we can try shocking your heart back into regular rhythm." He said they'd do what they could to schedule Dad for Friday morning, otherwise it would be Monday.

That afternoon we called Jim to let him know. He said he'd book a flight for Friday. Rachel had to return home that morning, but my youngest daughter, Jane, traveled from New York City to DC so that my other daughter, Sharon, could drive her out. They were able to swing by the airport and pick up their uncle on the way.

Jim and the girls wouldn't be there in time for the operation, so I went over to the hospital to be with Dad when they came to get him. The doctor said I could follow them down, and that there was a waiting room near the operating room. It did not seem long at all, and suddenly I saw them wheel Dad out. It was over so fast; I was sure that meant the procedure didn't work. I remained calm with an expression I hoped conveyed, "No sweat."

As they rolled him by the waiting room, Dad looked over at me. I smiled at him. He lifted his right hand and gave me the thumbs up sign.

"It worked?" I cried out, louder than was probably appropriate for a cardiology waiting room.

The doctor smiled and nodded. Dad was taken to the recovery room for a short while before they took him back to his room to rest. I took the opportunity to go home so I could be there when Jim and my girls arrived.

After updates, we all rode over to the hospital. Dad was in good spirits and happy to see his son and granddaughters. He was still tired so shooed us out of him room and said he'd see us the next day.

That evening I relaxed for the first time since Dad was admitted to the hospital. We laughed and told stories, and I enjoyed watching my daughters with my brother. We didn't see enough of one another, perhaps, but I was grateful that my children knew their aunts and uncles on both sides of their family. The regard they had for one another was evident.

We took turns going to the hospital so that we could get other things done during times someone else was taking a shift. At one point I was in Dad's room with my daughters when his primary care physician came in to visit. He sat in the window and talked to Dad. We began to ask questions. I noticed that my two daughters and I had him cornered. One sat next to him on the window seat, the other at the foot of the bed. I was near the door.

"My girls have you surrounded, Doctor," Dad said.

It occurred to me that Dad's army had mobilized once again. This time my platoon was at the front with him. I felt a lot better knowing that I had my team with me, everyone with a role, everyone with a job to do. And things were going well.

Since Dad was getting better, we decided that my brother and the girls would return home. Dad would be released within a few days. We could regroup by phone. We promised to call if we needed them.

Dad came home a little weak, but always the good patient. I did not have to consider Plan B. At least not yet.

CHAPTER 26

~

Cared For, Caretaker

*A*FTER SEVEN YEARS of living with my father, we've settled into a routine. Though at times there are missteps,
we recover quickly and move easily now, even gracefully,
as we dance together through life. If something or someone is out
of rhythm, we notice.

Most mornings I come downstairs to find the coffee started
and my mug on the counter, indicating that Dad's already gotten
his and is sitting in the den watching the news. Every now and
then, the kitchen is dark, the coffee is not ready, and the mugs
are not out. I always stop and take a deep breath. Then I go to
find him. Usually, I find that he slept late or that I've forgotten his
appointment for lab work, which requires that he not eat or drink
anything beforehand. Now I know to look first for his car before
heading up the stairs to his bedroom to see if he is still with me.

~

Typically, Dad goes upstairs at 8:00 each evening to wind down
by listening to a game on the radio before going to bed. I'm up a
little later, locking doors, turning off lights, finishing laundry or a
show before I head up, too.

I'm not sure why I changed the routine one night, but for some reason, I decided to stay downstairs later than normal to watch a movie. Normally, I'd have been upstairs and asleep when I heard a loud thump. I stopped to listen but heard nothing else. Probably a branch hitting the roof, I thought, as that is not unusual. Nothing. I headed upstairs.

By the time I got to the landing I thought I heard something else.

"Nancie."

I thought I could hear Dad calling me. I opened the door to his room and heard with more clarity: "Nancie."

Dad was lying on the floor next to his bed, his arm pinned under his right side.

"Dad, what happened?"

His voice was weak.

"I fell," he said. "I landed on my arm. I can't move or push myself up."

I am still amazed by how calm I was. Probably because this was about him. Not me. My focus was on the man on the floor. While I kneeled down and assessed the situation, I noted that he was speaking clearly, though his voice was weak. I asked him to tell me exactly what happened as I lifted him up and off his arm.

"Dad, can you get up if I help?"

"I can't move my right side."

I could have run immediately for my phone to call 911, but something told me it was important that he have as much control of this situation as he could.

"What do you want to do, Dad?"

"I guess we should go to the hospital. I'll need an ambulance."

"Calling now," I said, dialing my phone.

There it was. His decision. It wasn't that I didn't know we needed to call 911—I did. But it was his call to tell me to dial 911. Short of my being unconscious, I would want it to be my call, too, were I him. As I spoke to the operator, he said what I was about to say to her: "I think I've had a stroke."

By the time Dad got to the hospital, the feeling and ability to move his arm and leg had returned. So had his sense of humor. They admitted him and every day I'd hear laughter coming from his room as a nurse, doctor, or other staff member tended to him.

The MRI showed that the stroke had been serious given where it had occurred in his brain. But his recovery belied the seriousness. For a few days, there was a back and forth about whether or not he could have in-home care or would have to go to a rehabilitation facility. It seemed that every time I came in there was a different story. I was seldom there when they spoke to him and when I pressed for more details, he either didn't know or was confused.

There was confusion about his medications as well.

"Here," he'd say some days while handing me a bottle of pills. "They want me to take these now."

"'Did they say why?' I'd ask; or, "Do you take this in addition to the one you're already on?"

"I don't know," he'd respond.

Since I handled his medications at home, I'd look up any new prescriptions or changes in dosage. It was confusing for me, let alone someone recovering from a stroke. I asked the nurse for a copy of what they were administering. What they had did not match up with the list Dad's primary physician had given him. Their list contained medications he no longer took and omitted ones that had been prescribed before he was admitted to the hospital. We got everything updated.

One afternoon I came into his room and sensed he was upset. He was holding some brochures.

"What have you got there?" I took them from him. They were pamphlets from a residential facility.

"They want me to go to a place, but I don't want to. I don't think I need it."

I agreed with him. It was my opinion that though I was sure he might need some physical therapy for regaining strength and tips on maintaining his balance to prevent falls, all of that could be done at home or on an outpatient basis. As far as I knew he hadn't even had an assessment yet.

"Who spoke to you about this?" I asked.

"I don't know," he said.

I had a flashback to the last time he was in the hospital and watching the back of my daughter as she walked out of his room to the nurse's station and handed them the "Post-it Note". It was my turn.

"Okay," I said, "I'll be right back."

I approached the nurse's station, and the nurse smiled at me.

"Can you tell me who spoke with my father and gave him this information? And if they're in the hospital, I'd like to speak to them now or as soon as they are available. I want to make sure I understand what he was told."

The nurse immediately picked up the phone, and within minutes the patient coordinator arrived. The three of us huddled at the desk. I explained that he was not processing all the information they were giving him, not because he wasn't capable of understanding or wouldn't, but because he'd had a stroke, he was eighty-nine, he was on information-overload, *and* hard of hearing.

"People are walking in and out of the room, introducing themselves so fast and then talking to him about things that are new to him and don't necessarily relate to what the last person was talking to him about."

The patient coordinator and nurse both nodded and smiled. They were fantastic.

"I need you to speak to me, too, so I can make sure we both understand what he needs."

I told the patient coordinator that barring an assessment that contradicted my own, Dad could come home for in-home or out-patient care. She said there would be an assessment and that she thought from her observation that he would not need to be in a facility unless it was something he preferred.

I went back into Dad's room and let him know, then said, "Dad, I've told them that they have to talk to me, too, because I'm the one living with you and I want to make sure we're both on the same page so you can make the best decisions for you."

"Understood," he said. "Good idea."

Dad was released and we spent the next four months monitoring his vitals and weight each day. The doctors, physical therapists, pharmacists, and nurses to whom we conveyed his numbers each day were wonderful.

～

Less than a year after Dad's stroke, Dad fully recovered and is back to playing golf—though less frequently and using a cart rather than walking the course. He still goes to breakfast with the FOGs a few times a week when they're not teeing off.

Our overarching routine still exists, which relies on the both of us supporting it while still leaving enough time each day for our own interests and activities. We each have our chores, though I slowly—when he allows me to—relieve him of one or two at a time. I expect that to happen more and more.

I handle the housework, the grocery shopping, meals, and filling his pillboxes. He keeps track of what needs to be done—cars to the shop, when property and equipment maintenance needs to happen, how the furnace, water heater, and lawn mowers are working. I handle making the appointments. He drives his thirty-year-old pickup truck and me to the County Waste Transfer Station once a week, but now I empty the truck into the big containers by myself.

We still take a drive to the ocean or visit a different Eastern Shore town once a week whenever possible, but those trips are shorter now as he tires more easily.

His favorite activity is playing the slot machines at one of the nearby casinos. He wins. I lose. A disciplined gambler, he takes only so much money into the building with him, leaving his wallet and charge cards outside in the car. If I go with him, he gives me what he calls the "Flying Forty" because when I play it, "It just flies out the window."

Like the time I spend with him. It just seems to fly.

CHAPTER 27

~

Bridging the Divide

"**W**HEN DID YOU MOVE IN HERE?" Dad asks.

I calculate and then say, "Almost six years ago. Why?"

"Just wondered. That was quick."

"Time flies when you're having fun, Dad."

"Yes, it does. It's been good," he says.

Once I was asked to make a list of what I wanted out of life. The basics. If I could have what I wanted, what five things would they be? I listed the following:

My own family including children and grandchildren.
To live within thirty minutes of the ocean.
To be no more than four hours from New York City.
To travel.
To write full time and publish at least one book.

I share this with Dad.

"That's pretty good," he says. "You have what you wanted."

"And I have you," I tell him.

"Me and Fox News."

I grimace. "You had to mention that."

"You know, Dad. I've asked you a lot of questions, but I'm curious about one thing. How did you see me as a child?"

He looks a little startled and says, "What do you want to know that for?"

I'm immediately uncomfortable and sorry I asked. I've put him in an awkward situation. I stifled the urge to change the topic or laugh. I wait.

After a minute or two, just about the time I've given up that he'll answer, he surprises me and says, "You were my little sidekick," and smiles. "We were always together." We talk about that. I share some early memories I've carried around with me since childhood. He shares some of his.

There isn't much we can't talk about now. It's easier for me to share how I'm feeling, not just the good things, either, but when I'm sad, anxious, or afraid. Though there is one topic we try to avoid. We still can't discuss some things political for too long.

"They're trying to impeach Trump," he says, but I don't respond. "They can't impeach him. He didn't do anything," he continues. I try to divert him by discussing it generally. I try to move it away from the President to the presidency, something more general or operational.

"In some quarters there are thoughts about whether it makes sense for the country to do it. Whether it's good for the country."

"They've got nothing. Mueller's report said he was innocent."

"Actually, that's not quite what the report said."

"Yes, it did."

"Dad, did you read the report?" I know he hasn't. I open the car door and start to climb out.

"Yes, I did. Did you?" He knows I have.

"Oh, you did? When, Dad?" I ask as I head up the sidewalk, my back to him.

"None of your business," he says to my back.

"You didn't read it."

"When did you read it?" he challenges.

I lift my right arm up to the sky without turning around.

"Wait! Did you just throw me the bird? Did my daughter throw her father the bird?"

"Yes, Dad. Yes, I did."

"Wait till I tell your brothers," he says.

"Tell them I have one for them, too," I say, lifting my other arm. I hear my father start to laugh.

"That's nice," he says. "I'm going to tell the FOGs this, too."

Now I start to laugh.

EPILOGUE

Riding Shotgun

I ROLL DOWN THE WINDOW of my father's SUV and point the lens of my iPhone's camera toward a small portion of the landscape in front of me.

"Dad, do you mind slowing down?" I ask. "I want to take a picture."

Dad says nothing, but I know if I look, he'll be checking the rear and sideview mirrors before his foot hits the brake pedal as he pulls closer to the shoulder of the road.

We've just crossed the Wicomico River from Whitehaven on a cable ferry to Mount Vernon in Maryland (not George Washington's Mount Vernon in Virginia), just twenty miles from Salisbury, where I live with my father in the final house my parents bought and planned to live in between visits from their children, grandchildren, and hopefully, great-grandchildren. The house in which my mother died.

"Do you want me to stop?" he asks.

"Do you mind? I love this view. I've always wanted to come back and take a few shots of it," I tell him.

The first time we were here, about a year ago, there hadn't been time or, perhaps, I hadn't felt comfortable asking for the favor, so I didn't. I was afraid he might become impatient. Instead I made do and tried to capture everything in my mind in case I never made it back. Today it was more beautiful than I remembered.

"You've got it," he says, and pulls the car to a stop.

As I get out of the car, I pan the scene before me. There is so much to see. A narrow bend in the winding river hugged by a cluster of old clapboard houses. On the other side, tidal pools, sea grasses, different shades of blues ranging from sky blue to what a microbiology professor of mine once referred to as "Prussian blue" when describing the color of a stain on the slide we peered at, taking turns, through a microscope at some organism pressed between two slides decades ago. And the greens, mostly faded this late in summer.

"Take your time," Dad tells me. "We don't have anywhere to go."

Out of the corner of my eye while I walk back and forth trying to find the best shot, I catch him fiddling with his phone, turning up the volume on his satellite radio, and admiring the scenery himself.

On Saturday or Sunday mornings, Dad and I explore the Eastern Shore. He has calculated that we if we leave no later than 9:00 A.M. and drive no further than fifty-seven to seventy miles one way (based on the location of restaurants he'd like to try), there will be ample time to enjoy the sights, eat lunch or brunch, and return home in time to enjoy the rest of the afternoon in front of his television watching golf, baseball, or basketball, depending on the season. My father has to be on the move. He has a routine to follow, and on days when he doesn't get out to breakfast or golfing with his buddies or to play the slots at one of the local casinos, he gets antsy.

For me it's reminiscent of the drives we took on weekends or between transfers from one military post to another when I was a child—anywhere, no matter where we lived or traveled to. As a family we drove across Germany, Austria, and Italy. We drove from New York to California, from California to Texas, from Texas to Virginia, from Virginia to North Carolina. . . . So many days and miles in the car. Dad drove most of the time, except on long trips when Mom would spell him for an hour or two. A passenger then, I still am now.

I walk up and down the shoulder. I cannot decide where I should stand. How close in? How far out? At an angle? Standing? Kneeling? I resort to what I typically do when I'm confronted with too much to process or am overwhelmed: I change positions. I stand, kneel, squat, lean, twist, and flex, trying to find just the right place while I point and click, point and click, point and click in my attempts to not miss anything. I tell myself I can look through the images later, toss what I don't like or focus in and crop the images I do.

I walk back to the car.

"Done already? Are you sure? You can take your time, you know. Relax a little," my father cautions. "Make sure you get everything you want. There's no need to hurry."

"I got it," I say, hoping I did. I got something at least.

As he pulls back on to the road, I flip through the photos quickly, and one grabs my attention. In it, the ferry moves back across the river toward its ramp in front of the old houses on the Whitehaven riverside. Soft-edged tidal pools nestle among patches of vegetation, and seagull silhouettes dot a blue sky. And there, in the foreground, one perfectly placed, solitary stalk of seagrass stands among the others, caught mid-sway in the day's breeze, as though looking at the scene I see. Centered in the frame.

It's not a perfect picture. But it's close. I'm still new to this. All things get better with practice.

AKNOWLEDGEMENTS

A FRIEND TOLD ME that the acknowledgments were the hardest part of the book to write. For me, the writing of it is not hard, but the starting is. I have an army of people I could and should thank. But this section cannot be longer than the book, so I am forced to whittle the list down. I've tried to include anyone without whom this book—this specific book— would not have been written, let alone published.

This book has everything to do with family and is dedicated to my parents and my three daughters, and I feel I must expand on why. For Mom, because she knew when I was a toddler that words were my salve, read to me incessantly, and, when I was old enough, pushed me to search for the right ones, use them, then write them down. For Dad, who I've learned *was* always there, even if we didn't live together at the time, and who brought me home—sometimes kicking and screaming—before I knew I needed to be there. A huge thank you and apologies to Jim and Clint, my brothers, who I thought were my own babies from the time they came home from the hospital, despite the reminders to me that they were not. Thank you for being supportive and watching out for me. Thank you mostly for enduring my bossing you around as patiently as you did. It was bossiness in those cases, not assertiveness.

To my children. Carolyn Heilbrun spoke of mothers, our children, and the joy of "allowing ourselves, from time to time, to think of them as friends." My relationship to you individually and as a group is, perhaps, the greatest gift of my life.

To my first daughter, Rachel, who always said what she thought while growing up and has not allowed anything or anyone to stop her in that. It may be because in her truth-telling she is thoughtful, compassionate, and direct. She provided insights and perspectives during our conversations about the book that were invaluable. To my "middle," Sharon, whose own personal system for the documentation of dates, events, and specifics as to what transpired were essential to an accurate timeline. She was instrumental in validating or clarifying who was there and what was said. She also formatted the book for final submission to my editor, saving many sets of eyes. And, finally, to Jane, my youngest, who always listens, offers sage responses, suggests, and encourages—and unabashedly asks authors at the book readings she attends to sign their books and pass along their advice. I've received notes tucked inside those books with the words "just do it," "be brave," and "be honest." I have tried to be.

To my cousin John-Michael and his partner, Ray, who open their home as a way station every time I travel north for the book. They introduced me to burrata, Portuguese wines, Lantana trees, and their precious pup, Baci, who always seems happy to see me and sorry to see me leave.

I am so grateful to have many friends, all of whom have been there for me while I wrote *Tea with Dad*. To anyone not listed here, I'll be sending handwritten notes once this is over to those I could not mention but thought about.

My dear friend Debora Treu, whom I have known since Georgetown University, who read early chapters of the book and listened as I struggled through what to write and what to leave out. Here's to a return to Door County, Lucca, and Old Quebec City. I cannot wait until we can commence our explorations abroad again.

Acknowledgments

Thank you to alpha and beta readers Marian Hochberg, Sylvia Lacock, Rene Ebert, Virginia Parker, David Feldman, LouAnn Watkins Clark, Jerilyn Dufresne, Joanne Giulietti, Kiersten Aschauer, Maria Trimarchi, Erin Sullivan, Trish Barber, and Heather Perram Frank. I took everything you told me and tried to make the book better.

To Clare Grana, whose home is always open when I need a retreat and who lends me an office and all the office supplies and fancy equipment I need when I work there. She gives me the most comfortable guest room in the world, good food, wine, and her voice, saying, "Yes. I remember. I was there."

And to Bonnie Rick who—no matter what she has been through—has always been present for me and has been in my life consistently and longer than any other friend I have ever known and loved. For all that friendship entails.

There would not be a book at all if it had not been for the experience created by Steve Eisner and the staff at the When Words Count Retreat—that cozy Vermont inn geared to writers that I was headed to on that ill-fated Amtrak train—as well as the women I met during my stays there.

I must mention the members of my happy hour and Pitch Week cohort: Beth Bruce Russell, Ellen Mulligan, Elise Von Holten, Jane VanVooren Rogers, and Sue Roulusonis. Thanks for the wines, the whines, and unfailing support you shared with me. When writing got difficult, I'd imagine you in that room with the fire, listening to me read.

To my newest writing friend, Barbara Newman, one of the most beautiful souls and loving human beings I have the gift of knowing. Thank you for our almost daily "How are you doing?" "Get back to it!" and "Let's have tea." I cannot wait to read your book when it's done. The world is waiting for it.

And to all the professionals who have helped me through the process of pushing this book out into the world: Peg Moran, my first line editor, and Asha Hossain, for beautiful book cover concepts.

To Ken Sherman of Ken Sherman & Associates, for nailing my subtitle and the feel of the book cover, and for the urgency behind his advice to be courageous and tell the real story when I held back.

To my lovely writing coach during the time I pitched my book, author Judith Krummeck, for your guidance, support, and assurance.

To Ben Tanzer, novelist, essayist, podcaster, and principal at Heft Creative Strategies, who said, "You present all 'Merchant and Ivory,' but underneath it, there's a mess. I want to read about that." I tried. I'm so excited to work with you to bring this book out into the world.

Finally, to Green Writers Press: Dede Cummings, my publisher (and a wonderful poet), who opened the door to the perfect home for my first book—a home with a mission and a value system I cherish. To Sarah Ellis, not just for her wonderful copyedits, but for her comments as a reader of this book. To Ferne Johansson, who—during her search for errant punctuation, proper word usage, style consistencies, and all things that need fixing in a manuscript—discovered treasures of which I was not aware and showed me how to share them.

Last and especially, to my editor, Emma Irving, who understood what this book was about from the beginning, told me so, then trusted my instincts and gently, yet firmly, kept me on course. I owe you so much, and I am grateful.

ABOUT THE AUTHOR

NANCIE LAIRD YOUNG lives on the Eastern Shore of Maryland where she writes when not competing with her father for who takes care of whom or "discussing" politics. As a military brat she traveled in Europe, the Far East, and across the United States with her family. She graduated from Georgetown University with concentrations in English Literature and Organizational Behavior and made her way through most of an MBA. She has written about the early days of the internet and worked at washingtonpost.com, LifetimeTV.com, and AOL/Time Warner.